GOD PROMISE TO THE CHINESE

GOD'S PROMISE TO THE CHINESE

Ethel R. Nelson
Richard E. Broadberry

Published by Read Books
2014

Cover Illustration of Emperor Yao by Shunichi Yamamato
Cover Design by Robert Mason

Originally published as *Mysteries Confucius Couldn't Solve,* © 1986 Ethel R. Nelson. Revised 1994 (Concordia Publishing House) as *Genesis and the Mystery Confucius Couldn't Solve.*

5th Printing

Copyright © 1997 Ethel R. Nelson

Read Books Publisher, a division of Christian Heritage Media
P.O. Box 171
Berrien Springs, MI 49103

ISBN-13: 978-0-937869-04-8

Dedication

To our beloved spouses,
        Roger Nelson and
        Maggie Broadberry

Contents

Foreword and Acknowledgments ix

Preface by Dr. Samuel Wang...xi

1 Confucius Revealed the Clue 1

2 Who Is ShangDi?...7

3 In the Beginning—God..15

4 Chinese Concepts of Mankind's Creation................23

5 Secrets of a Lost Garden...31

6 Invader in the Garden...41

7 The Fatal Bite 47

8 A Costly Rescue Plan 55

9 Confucius Pointed the Way......................................63

10 The Seed of the Woman 73

11 Original Purpose of the Altar of Heaven 83

12 ShangDi's Last Promise 93

Epilog: Synchronizing Chinese and Biblical History....105

References 121

Bibliography..133

Character Index...135

Foreword and Acknowledgments

About 1968 I picked up a little book entitled *Genesis and the Chinese* by C.H. Kang. I never dreamed this subject would eventually be a consuming interest, for my initial response to the title was "no connection!" But upon opening the book, my curiosity was immediately piqued. I began using selected Chinese characters in my Bible studies with persons in Bangkok, Thailand where I then worked as a medical pathologist in a large mission hospital. Nearly ten years later I finally met C.H. Kang, by then quite elderly. The eventual result of our friendship was publication of *Discovery of Genesis* (Concordia Publishing House, 1979).

I soon became determined to confirm the idea that the ancient Chinese had indeed possessed an unusual knowledge of sacred history, which they had incorporated into their written language. To authenticate the study, therefore, I needed to delve into the more ancient forms of the characters—the seal and bronzeware characters. Pastor Kang, gave me a book to use as I began the investigation. As a result of the publication of *Discovery of Genesis,* I received many letters, among these, a letter from Richard Broadberry, living in Taipei, and also working in the medical field. As he began making significant contributions to a new manuscript then in preparation, I invited him to be my co-author.

As we neared completion of the book, Richard became convinced after talking with a curator at the Palace Museum in Taipei, that we should include a study of the oracle bone writing. This oracle bone writing is the most ancient known Chinese writing, and therefore carries the most authentic original thought. It was an excellent decision to include it in *Mysteries Confucius Couldn't Solve* (Read Books Publisher, 1986), published in both English and Chinese.

With my retirement from the active practice of medicine, I had more time to devote to the fascinating Chinese character research. The result for Richard and myself was a revised and enlarged book entitled *Genesis and the Mystery Confucius Could't Solve* (Concordia, 1994).

God's Promise to the Chinese (Read Books, 1996) was the next updated book. *Oracle Bones Speak* (Read Books, 2011) is the same book, only it is bilingual, with English and Chinese side by side. To our minds, this present book is a good confirmation of our proposed "hieroglyphic" interpretation of Chinese characters.

Ethel R. Nelson, M.D.

Preface

The Chinese are everywhere! A Chinese migratory wave anciently brought the Chinese into every corner of the world. This phenomenon seems to echo, in a strong and interesting way, God's promise, "And God blessed them, and said unto them, Be fruitful, and multiply, and replenish the earth" (Genesis 1:26).

It is a well-known fact that the Chinese civilization is one of the oldest in the world, and that China may be the only nation that enjoys an unbroken history from antiquity to our contemporary world. However, a humanistic approach has dominated studies and understanding of the rich and extensive history of China. Many have lost sight of the righteous and godly traditions as found in her rich, long, and glorious history. Biblical scholars have almost unanimously turned their attention to the Near East in discovering the biblical world, forgetting that the REAL biblical world actually includes the WHOLE world and beyond. Ancient China was certainly an integral part of the "Biblical world". Studies into her ancient culture enrich one's understanding of the Bible and the unsearchable love of God.

God's Promise to the Chinese is an intriguing historical study. The authors delve into the "Oracle Bone" inscriptions written on bones or tortoise shells. These are the earliest pictographic Chinese writings known to us today. Here one discovers enormous, exciting evidences that God's promises were also once given to the ancient Chinese. They devised vivid ways to keep and pass on this treasure to their descendants through their Chinese "character-writing". Incidentally, Chinese characters are probably the only ancient writing that is still in use today.

Readers will be fascinated to learn that before the written Bible appeared, the word of God was transmitted from generation to generation by word-of-mouth. Oral tradition existed for the first twenty-five hundred years of human history. In other words, an oral version of the Bible was circulated in each generation before the written version came to light.

Obviously, there would be similarities and differences between the two versions. For instance, the Eden story, the flood, and the Tower of Babel incidents may be found in both. However, in the oral version one would not be able to find the story of Abraham, Moses, or David, because some of those who were scattered from the Tower of Babel would not have known about them after they were sent off to other parts of the world.

Are there evidences in Chinese culture which show that the early Chinese were taught the stories of the creation, the temptation, the fall, or the flood in the same way as recorded in the beginning chapters of the written scriptures? Did they record anything about the plan of salvation through Jesus Christ the Son of God? How would they relate to the Lamb of God which takes away the sins of the world? Could there be witnesses left by God for the Chinese throughout her long history? The authors expertly and succinctly have dug out from the vast storehouse of oracle bone writings convincing materials that lead to surprising, eye-opening insights and conclusions. Readers will be awed to say with the authors, "That was the true Light, which lighteth every man that cometh into the world." (John 1:9)

There is a perplexingly interesting contradiction that exists in the Christian world. People normally understand that the gospel was first proclaimed in Genesis 3:15 in the garden of Eden. However, the same group seem to trace the history of Christianity for only 2000 years. Sadly, such a contradiction has gone by unnoticed for too long! It is time to realize that the religion of the disciples of Jesus was the same as that of Adam. The religion as recorded by the Jewish prophets in the written scriptures was similar to that passed on to the ancient Chinese through oral tradition. The God of Abraham is the same God as that of the ancient Chinese, the Creator God of Adam and the entire universe. In this book, the authors have done a remarkable job of providing ample evidence through their reasonable analyses. Their conclusions will stand the most rigid scrutinizing.

For the Christian world, this book will continue to be an eye-opener to the amazing grace of God. For the modern Chinese who have somewhat lost their wonderful spiritual heritage, this book will certainly be a milestone work to call them back to the God their ancestors have served for ages, and to prepare them to receive the abundant blessings through God's promise to the Chinese.

Samuel Wang, D. Miss.

Confucius Revealed the Clue

For more than 4,000 years the reigning emperors of China traveled annually to the border of their country or to the imperial city. There, on an outdoor altar, they sacrificed and burned young unblemished bullocks to their God, *ShangDi* (上帝), whose name means literally the *God* 帝 *above* 上, or *Supreme God.*

The Border Sacrifice (郊祀), as this ceremony came to be called, was a ceremony conducted in continuous sequence ever since the legendary period of Chinese history, before the first dynastic rule which began in 2205 B.C. Unfortunately, the Border Sacrifice became closely identified with the rulership of China, for the emperor himself, acting as high priest, was the chief participant in the ceremony. Consequently, when the Manchus were deposed in 1911 of our own century, not only did the dynastic reign end forever, but so did China's longest celebrated and most colorful sacrifice: the Border Sacrifice. So important to the mind of the great philosopher Confucius

(551-479 B.C.) was this Border Sacrifice that he compared a comprehension of the ritual to the efficient ruling of the Chinese empire.

> He who understands the ceremonies of the sacrifices to Heaven and Earth . . .would find the government of a kingdom as easy as to look into his palm![1]

Why did Confucius attach so much significance to this ancient Border Sacrifice? You will find the answer to this question as you read on!

One of the earliest accounts of the Border Sacrifice is found in the *Shu Jing (Book of History)*,[2] compiled by Confucius himself, where it is recorded of Emperor Shun (c. 2230 B.C.) that "he sacrificed to ShangDi."[3] From an early date, the Chinese were already offering sacrifices to ShangDi on an altar of earth on the top of Mount Tai in Shan-Dong, at the eastern border of China. A border sacrifice at an eastern locale is most significant, as we shall subsequently learn.

In the 15th century A.D., this important sacrifice was moved to the southern part of Beijing, where an extensive Altar of Heaven complex came to quarter three main sacred edifices. Each is laid out on a north-south axis, joined by a paved way. The northernmost structure, the Hall of Prayer for Good Harvests, was originally built in 1420, then rebuilt in the late 19th century after lightning caused it to be burned. Its circular hall with three layers of eaves rises upwards in its cone-shaped tiered roof, its deep blue tiles mirroring the sky above. The terrace it stands on consists of three circular levels of marble, each bounded with carved balustrades.

To the south is a second, smaller building, called the Imperial Vault of Heaven. Built in 1530, its architectural plan is similar to the Hall of Prayer, raised also upon a marble stone foundation with balustrades. Inside this edifice resides no religious images. A tablet on the north wall (also found in the Hall of Prayer) is inscribed with the characters 皇天上帝 (*Heavenly Sovereign ShangDi*), clearly indicating that ShangDi was the God they worshiped in the Border Sacrifice.

In a straight line, yet farther south, is the altar of sacrifice itself. This great, triple-tiered, white marble Altar of Heaven, 75 meters (250 feet) in diameter, again surrounded on each level by balustrades, is an imposing structure. The uppermost level can be reached by a series of steps on each of four sides. A monumental undertaking, construction of it was completed in 1539.

Transport yourself back in time to observe firsthand the events surrounding ancient China's most sacred site and rite. As the winter solstice (about December 22) approaches, the supporting cast taking part in this ceremony readies itself for the glorious ritual. Singers prepare their colorful silken robes; musicians dust off their racks of suspended bronze bells, varying-sized drums, cymbals, flutes, and stringed instruments, dedicated exclusively for use in this annual event.

On the morning before the winter solstice, the emperor, the "Son of Heaven," in gorgeous array passes through the front gate of the Imperial Palace (the Forbidden City) and makes his way in a procession to the Altar of Heaven complex. An impressive retinue of princes and high officials follows. The streets of Beijing are silent, as all residents are required to remain hidden behind shuttered windows.

By reviewing the litany of the Statutes of the Ming Dynasty (大明會典)in which the prayers and hymns of praise used in this ceremony are recorded, one may begin to understand the Chinese reverence for ShangDi. After arriving at the Altar of Heaven complex, the emperor first meditates in the Imperial Vault, while the costumed singers, accompanied by the musicians, sing the recitation:

> To Thee, O mysteriously–working Maker, I look up in thought. How imperial is the expansive arch (where Thou dwellest).... With the great ceremonies I reverently honour Thee. Thy servant, I am but a reed or willow; my heart is but as that of an ant; yet have I received Thy favouring decree, appointing me to the government of the empire. I deeply cherish a sense of my ignorance and blindness, and am afraid, lest I prove unworthy of Thy great favours. Therefore will I observe all the rules and statutes, striving, insignificant as I am, to discharge my loyal duty. Far distant here, I look up to Thy heavenly palace. Come in Thy precious chariot to the altar. Thy servant, I bow my head to the earth reverently, expecting Thine abundant grace. All my officers are here arranged along with me, joyfully worshipping before Thee.... Oh that Thou wouldest vouchsafe to accept our offerings, and regard us, while thus we worship Thee, whose goodness is inexhaustible![4]

The emperor then makes his way to the Hall of Prayer for Good Harvests.

On the next day's festive solstice, the emperor returns to the Imperial Vault. He then proceeds to the Round Altar (of Heaven) to perform the sacrificial rituals, the most important part of the ceremony. The crisp morning air is filled with songs of praise and prayer. (Some of these will be presented at appropriate points in subsequent chapters). Gems and silks are brought forth, as well as vessels of food, and three offerings of wine, all accompanied by music and dances:

> The dances have all been performed, and nine times the music has resounded. Grant, O Te [Di], Thy great blessing to increase the happiness of my house. The instruments of metal and precious stones have given out their melody. The jeweled girdles of the officers have emitted their tinklings.... While we celebrate His great name, what limit can there be, or what measure? For ever He setteth fast the high heavens, and establisheth the solid earth. His government is everlasting. His unworthy servant, I bow my head, I lay it in the dust, bathed in His grace and glory.[5]

Lastly, after the sacrificial bullock has been slaughtered on the Altar of Heaven, it is burned, and a final song resounds:

> We have worshipped and written the Great Name on this gem–like sheet. Now we display it before Te, [Di] and place it in the fire. These valuable offerings of silks and fine meats we burn also with these sincere prayers, that they may ascend in volumes of flames up to the distant azure. All the ends of the earth look up to Him. All human beings, all things on the earth, rejoice together in the Great Name.[6]

Today the Temple and Altar of Heaven (Tian Tan) in Beijing are prime tourist attractions. However, few people in the surging crowds that clamber over the worn marble steps even concern themselves with wondering about the origin and meaning of the great Border Sacrifice[7] that used to be performed there. But centuries ago, the important ceremony that inspired the construction of these beautiful edifices was recognized by Confucius as representing perhaps the emperor's single most responsible act of obedience to the ultimate Ruler of all, the Supreme God in Heaven, ShangDi.

Is it possible that we can trace the original intention of this magnificent ceremony of antiquity? We believe so—and by a most unusual means. We will find, strangely enough, that even though the ritual is no longer practiced in China today, it still has great significance for all—for those of the Western world as well as Asia.

2

Who Is ShangDi?

Do you ever wonder where you came from? Most people do. Some even have a well-kept family record of ancestors, covering many generations. Regardless of whether or not you know who your ancestors were, do you have any idea how humanity and all life on earth came into being or who the very first human beings were?

Some scientists today tell us that humanity has evolved through countless ages from lower forms of life. They say people emerged as upright creatures, descendants of an apelike animal. However, did you know that the ancient teachings of the Chinese reveal that the first man and woman on earth were stately, intelligent, specially created beings? They even resembled their great Creator God, ShangDi. According to the Chinese, ShangDi (上帝) made not only people, but the earth and all life in it, as well as the entire universe.

In fact, as mentioned in the last chapter, ShangDi, means the *Supreme God* 上帝 and indicates His *Supreme Rulership* in heaven. Since the Zhou Dynasty, the name ShangDi has been used interchangeably with *Heaven, God* (天). In the last chapter we also found that from the most remote time in Chinese history, the sacred Border Sacrifice was conducted each year for the worship of ShangDi. As the emperor himself took part in this annual service dedicated to ShangDi, the following words, recorded in the collected Statutes of the Ming Dynasty (大明會典), were recited, clearly showing that ShangDi is the Creator of the world:

> Of old in the beginning, there was the great chaos, without form and dark. The five elements [planets] had not begun to revolve, nor the sun and moon to shine. You, O Spiritual Sovereign [神皇] first divided the grosser parts from the purer. You made heaven. You made earth. You made man. All things with their reproducing power got their being.[1]

ShangDi's continuing regard and love for His created beings are further demonstrated in other recitations from the Border Sacrifice ceremony:

> All the numerous tribes of animated beings are indebted to Thy favour for their beginnings. Men and things are all emparadised in Thy love, O Te [Di]. All living things are indebted to Your goodness, but who knows from whom his blessings come to him? You alone, O Lord, are the true parent of all things.[2]

> He [ShangDi] sets fast forever the high heaven, and establishes the solid earth. His government is everlasting.[3]

Your sovereign goodness cannot be measured. As a potter, You have made all living things.[4]

From the foregoing we learn that ShangDi made the heavens and the earth and people. He is the true parent of all things. His love is over all His works. His years are without end. His goodness cannot be measured. This is what the ancient Chinese believed. Could this be the truth?

Said Confucius in the *Zhong Yong (Doctrine of the Mean),* "The ceremonies of the celestial and terrestrial sacrifices are those by which men serve ShangDi."[5]

Actually there eventually came to be two border sacrifices. The offering to Heaven at the winter solstice on the southern border, representing ShangDi's divine majesty, gradually became the more important. At the summer solstice, a sacrifice to the earth, representative of His divine care, was observed on the northern border.[6]

Did ShangDi die along with the imperial reign in China in 1911? The Chinese today certainly are not ignorant of ShangDi, but few really appreciate Him as the original God of China, the Creator of heaven and earth. Is it possible that though unknown and unappreciated, ShangDi is still the supreme ruler, not only of the Chinese, but over all of earth's inhabitants, since He created them all?

Historically, the Shang Dynasty's (1766-1122 B.C.) recognition of ShangDi as the true Supreme God over all gods may have continued into the Zhou Dynasty (1122-255 B.C.), but by the Han Dynasty (206 B.C.-24 A.D.), ShangDi was largely forgotten. Buddhism and Taoism, in addition to the interwoven religion of ancestor-worship, predominated. However, all traces and knowledge of the original God of China have not been erased. We believe a beautiful history of the beginnings of the human race on the newly created planet earth have been perfectly preserved in the ancient character-writing of the Chinese language. The written language was invented simultaneously with the development of the early Chinese culture.

According to tradition, during the reign of the Yellow Emperor Huang Di, the first characters, simple drawings of familiar objects, were invented.[7] Picture words (pictographs) were the earliest form of writing in the ancient world. Other peoples living at the same time in Egypt and Sumer also had their own pictographic writing. During the Shang dynasty, the Chinese writing consisted of simple pictographs as well as compound pictographs, some with phonetic association.

Of course, in order to be meaningful, the compound pictographs would have to be based upon concepts or knowledge commonly held and understood by these ancient people. Familiar historical events of a sacred nature (such as the creation of the first man and woman, the original loving relationship between God and people, how this relationship was broken, and God's remedy to restore it) appear to have been the subjects of great interest and were, therefore, incorporated into such graphs—as we shall see.

Once these specific characters had been invented and accepted, they appear to have gradually lost their original historical connections. With the passage of century after century, the origin and accurate meaning of these characters were lost or became blurred, even as the true identity of ShangDi also became misunderstood.

To add to the difficulty in analyzing the characters for their true meanings, scribes through the centuries expressed the ideas of the characters with stylistic variations, thus producing many ways of writing a single character. There have been continuing modifications since then, so that most of today's characters are quite different from the early pictographs.

For this reason, we will examine the most ancient character forms, known as the oracle bone writing, to learn the original intention and meanings. On these bone artifacts, the characters are clear pictographs that can be more easily deciphered than today's writing forms. These "oracle bone" characters, incised on bones and tortoise shell plastrons, were used for divination purposes, hence their name.

The first dictionary to analyze the original meaning of Chinese characters was the *Shuo-Wen Chieh-tzu,* compiled by Xu Shen and presented to the throne in A.D. 121.[8] Most Chinese dictionaries are still based upon the *Shuo Wen.* However, this material shows few Shang or oracle bone examples.

Also, by Xu Shen's day, Taoist ideas had almost completely replaced the original ancient religious beliefs in a single Creator God, ShangDi. Xu Shen naturally analyzed the characters according to the current knowledge and thinking of his day. Since the original intentions of the inventor had long since been buried in the dust of passing ages, how could the true ideas behind many of the ancient characters ever be recovered? Ironically, time itself has archaeologically uncovered from the same dust excavated oracle bone writings of almost 3500 years ago which provide the answers.

In 1899 a specialist in Chinese writing discovered, in a Chinese herbal shop, oracle bones containing an ancient script. These bones were being ground and used for medicine. Their source was traced to a site in Anyang, Henan Province. Since then over 150,000 specimens have been uncovered.[9]

The idea of comparing certain Chinese ancient graphs with another extremely old historical document, the sacred writings of the Hebrew people, has produced startling results. One of the purposes of this book is to bring together and demonstrate the similarity of the historical narratives of the two widely separated Chinese and Hebrew ancient civilizations.

Were many of the Chinese pictographs drawn from objects and activities of everyday life, or were they more specifically oriented to the ancients' knowledge of sacred history? We now believe that the ancient Chinese written characters were "hieroglyphic"—"hiero" indicating "sacred," and "glyph" meaning "engraving." By the end of this book, you will be better able to judge the merits of the "hieroglyphic" system here introduced.

From earliest human memory and tradition, as well as through inspiration from the God of the Hebrews, a prophet, Moses, recorded the beginnings of earth's history. The first book of the Hebrew Scriptures is called Genesis: "Beginnings." This oldest of the Hebrew narratives was written about 1500 B.C., more than 200 years *after* the start of the Shang Dynasty which produced the earliest extant Chinese writing, the oracle bone inscriptions.

It is indeed interesting to examine the recitations used in the Chinese Border Sacrifice rites worshiping ShangDi and compare them with the first verses of the Hebrew Genesis, which also name the Creator God. Read again these recitations given at the beginning of the chapter (p. 8), and note the similarity with excerpts from the more detailed story as recorded in the Hebrew writings:

> In the beginning God created the heavens and the earth. The earth was without form, and void; and darkness was on the face of the deep....
>
> Then God said, "Let the waters under the heavens be gathered together into one place, and let the dry land appear"; and it was so. And God called the dry land Earth, and the gathering together of the waters He called Seas....
>
> Then God made two great lights: the greater light to rule the day, and the lesser light to rule the night. He made the stars also....
>
> So God created man in His own image;... male and female He created them. Then God blessed them, and God said to them, "Be fruitful and multiply; fill the earth and subdue it; have dominion over the fish of

the sea, over the birds of the air, and over every living thing that moves on the earth."[10]

ShangDi, the Creator God of the Chinese, surely appears to be one and the same as the Creator God of the Hebrews. In fact, one of the Hebrew names for God was El Shaddai, phonetically similar to ShangDi. Even more similar is the Early Zhou pronunciation of ShangDi which is "djanh-tigh" [Zhandai].[11]

Because the oracle bone script is the oldest extant Chinese writing, we will use these characters exclusively in this book. Let us now begin an investigation of earth's earliest history by analyzing oracle bone characters. At the same time, we will compare stories contained in them with the ancient Hebrew narratives.

3

In the Beginning — God

"In the beginning" is a phrase used in both the Chinese (p. 8) and Hebrew (p. 13) texts to show that the Creator-God *predated* all else. The Chinese Border Sacrifice recitation reads:

> Of old, in the *beginning* there was the great chaos. . .
> You, O Spiritual Sovereign. . .made heaven. You made
> earth. You made man.... [1]

The Hebrew Genesis 1:1 states:

> In the *beginning* God created the heavens and the
> earth. [2]

Another name for their God which the ancient Chinese used interchangeably with ShangDi was Heaven (Tian, see p. 8). This is clearly shown in the oracle bone inscriptions, and later stated by Zheng Xuan, a scholar of the early Han dynasty who said, "ShangDi is another name for Heaven (Tian)." [3] The great philosopher Motze (408-382 B.C.) also thought of Heaven (Tian) as the Creator-God:

> I know *Heaven* loves men dearly not without reason.
> *Heaven* ordered the sun, the moon, and the stars to

enlighten and guide them. *Heaven* ordained the four seasons, Spring, Autumn, Winter, and Summer, to regulate them. *Heaven* sent down snow, frost, rain, and dew to grow the five grains and flax and silk so that the people could use and enjoy them. *Heaven* established the hills and rivers, ravines and valleys, and arranged many things to minister to man's good or bring him evil.[4]

Heaven (Tian) is the Creator-God of whom Motze spoke. Today, *Heaven* (天) is more often thought of as the sky, or starry heavens, but as apparent from the early writing 天 , 大 ,[5] Heaven represented not a place, but Someone *Great, Noble* 大 [6] (大) from *above* 二 [7] (上).

Heaven, God
Tian

great, noble

above

大 + 二 = 天

great, noble　　　*above*　　　*Heaven, God*

Supreme God,
Di, (ShangDi)

to manifest,
show, pro-
claim, exhibit

Recall that ShangDi is designated as the Supreme God. From the oracle bone character of *Di, God* 禾 , 禾 [8] (帝), we learn that this God 禾 comes from *above* 二 (上). Likewise, the *Noble* 大 Person in *Heaven* 天 (天), also "coming from above," 二 is God. The character, *Di* 禾 (帝), will be better appreciated and fully analyzed later in this book.

In the character 丅 , 丅 , 示 [9] (示) meaning *to manifest, show, proclaim, exhibit,* we find a prophecy or revelation. The symbol 丨 [10] (十) indicates both *ten* and *complete,* but must also represent a "complete," therefore "perfect," Person coming down from *above* 二 (上). This Person

16

"manifested" the divine characteristics of God while a man on earth, being perfect and sinless.

丨	+	二	=	丅
complete (Person)		*above*		*to manifest*

The Creator-God who became a man was designated by the ancient Chinese as the *Head, Beginning, Principal* 页 [11] (元): a *Person* 亻 [12] (人) from *above* 二 (上).

亻	+	二	=	页
Person		*above*		*Beginning, First, Head*

This heavenly Person is further described in the later record of the Hebrew people:

> In the *beginning* was the Word, and the Word was with God, and the Word was God. He was *in the beginning* with God. All things were made through Him, and without Him nothing was made that was made.... And the word *became flesh and dwelt among us*....[13]

The God-Man further described Himself:

> "I am the Alpha and the Omega, the *Beginning* and the End," says the Lord, "who is and who was and who is to come, the Almighty."[14]

These are mysterious words which the ancient Chinese characters will further expand upon.

The Hebrew Creator-God consists of three Persons known as the "Godhead" or "Trinity." Although three separate Persons are represented, the Members of the Godhead function as one in purpose and character. They are God the Father, God the Son, and God the Holy Spirit. How fascinating that the origi-

ten, complete

First, Principal, Head, Beginning

Person

17

nal Chinese concept of God was exactly the same! In 示 (示) we find that this *Complete* | Person from *above* — represented not only Himself, but also all three perfect | + 丅 + | Members of the Godhead. Much more will be said , as we proceed, about this important Member of the Godhead who came to earth to *show* what God was really like. We find that 丅 , 丁 is the most primitive symbol for the "*manifestation of God*," hence we have termed it the "God radical."

$$ |/\backslash \quad + \quad = \quad = \quad 示 $$

3 complete	*above*	*to manifest, show*
(Persons)		*("God Radical")*

rain, "Holy Spirit"

Thus far we have met four characters representing the God of Heaven: *Di* 帝 (帝); *Heaven* 天 (天); *Beginning, First* 元 (元); and *manifest* 示 (示). There is yet another important character used by the Chinese: *rain* 雨 [15] (雨), which certainly does come down from *above* — . However, might this graph have originally had an additional meaning? Indeed, the Early Zhou meaning for this graph is "to fall from heaven," and it could well apply to the Holy Spirit, the third Member of the Godhead. The Holy Spirit also descends from *above* — (上), but is Agent for all three *complete* ||| Persons of the Trinity. We will subsequently learn the important symbolism for the "*water* 水 [16] (水) of life."

water

$$ = \quad + \quad ||| \quad + \quad 水 \quad = \quad 雨 $$

above	*3 complete (Persons)*	*water*	*rain*

How interesting that the Hebrew Scriptures too symbolize the Holy Spirit by rain:

> And rejoice in the Lord your God; For He has given you the *former rain* faithfully, And He will cause the *rain* to come down for you—the *former rain*, and the latter *rain* in the first month. . . .I will pour out *My Spirit in those days.* . . .[17]

Again in the character, *drops of rain* ^{○○○} [18](霝),the raindrops ^{◇◇◇} have the appearance of flames. (See ∨, p. 24). This is not a coincidence for when the Holy Spirit was manifested on earth in a special way, some 2,000 years ago, this was referred to as "tongues of fire." We read:

raindrops

> . . .they were all with one accord in one place. And suddenly there came a sound from heaven, as of a rushing mighty wind, and it filled the whole house where they were sitting. Then there appeared to them *tongues, as of fire,* and one sat upon each of them. And they were all filled with the *Holy Spirit*. . . [19]

Does the apparent Chinese knowledge of God that coincides so closely with the Hebrew Scriptures have significance? We will pursue the idea further.

From oracle bone characters such as these, we can recover the ancient understanding regarding the origin and identity of ShangDi. As we have learned, the Border Sacrifice to ShangDi clearly identifies Him as the Creator-God of the universe. The next question is, how did ShangDi create all things? Note one further recitation from this ancient Border Sacrifice rite:

> When Te [Di], the Lord, had so decreed, He called into existence [originated] heaven, earth, and man.

> Between heaven and earth He separately placed in order men and things, all overspread by the heavens.[20]

Notice that ShangDi, according to the ancient Chinese record, *commanded* into existence heaven, earth, and man. Compare this with the way the Hebrew text describes the method of creation by El Shaddai, who, we suspect, is identical with ShangDi (p. 14), as the similarity in name and role would suggest:

> The Lord created the heavens by His *command*, the sun, moon, and stars by His spoken word....When He spoke, the world was created; at His *command* everything appeared.[21]

The Chinese and Hebrew records are identical, again proving that the Creator-God of both the Chinese and Hebrews are one and the same. El Shaddai (ShangDi) simply spoke objects into being. Plants and animals sprang into being at His command.

But most wonderful of all, according to the Hebrew Scriptures, His whole creative work of producing not only our earth but also the whole planetary system out of nothing took but six ordinary 24-hour days.

A summary of the Hebrew Genesis reveals that, on the first day, El Shaddai (ShangDi) created light. The second day, He divided the waters surrounding the earth and in this space created the atmospheric heavens with their life-supporting gases. The third day, He pushed back the waters over portions of the earth and formed seas. Upon the dry land that appeared, He brought forth vegetation with plants yielding seed to reproduce themselves. At the close of each day He saw that everything was good.

The fourth day, El Shaddai (ShangDi) made the sun, moon, and planets and set them in motion in the heavens to produce the days, months, and seasons. On the fifth day, He brought forth swarms of living creatures in the seas and birds in the skies. All creatures were given reproductive powers.

The sixth day, He said, "Let the earth bring forth the living creature according to its kind ... and it was so."[22]

to produce, bring forth, create, life

Here, El Shaddai (ShangDi) commanded the earth to bring forth living animals. An oracle bone form of the radical *to produce, bring forth, create* 〔23〕(生) shows God with arms upraised and the *earth* ___ (土). We will confirm the previously unrecognized symbol as "God" more conclusively later.

$$\text{God} + \text{earth} = \text{to produce, bring forth, create}$$

| "God" | earth | to produce, bring forth, create |

to speak, tell

Furthermore, the character *to speak, to tell* 〔24〕(告) combines *to create* with a *mouth* 〔25〕(口). Contained within this one character, we find all the elements of creation: God creates from the earth ___ by speaking, with His mouth.

mouth

$$\text{God} + \text{earth} = \text{create} + \text{mouth} = \text{to speak, tell}$$

| "God" | earth | create | mouth | to speak, tell |

21

The foregoing is an illustration demonstrating how an "idea-in-writing" character was cleverly formed. The most primitive symbols, often simple pictures, have come down as today's "radicals," the building blocks of the written language. As previously stated, since the ancient forms are more pictographic, and the oracle bone characters are the most ancient known forms, they will be used exclusively in this book, with today's renditions in parenthesis, e.g., 屮 （告）.

Once again, we'd like to explain our format used throughout the book. Dictionary definitions of characters are italicized, whereas definitions occasionally assigned by the authors are placed in quotes or are unitalicized .

As we continue our study, we will increasingly appreciate how the Chinese people have indeed been blessed by a unique revelation inspired by the God of heaven Himself, ShangDi.

Chinese Concepts of Mankind's Creation

The first human being on earth, according to both the Chinese and Hebrew records, was a fully grown adult man who came forth from the hands of God. In the Hebrew Scriptures, this is the record of man's creation:

God, Heaven

> Then God [Elohim] said: "And now We will make human beings; they will be like Us and resemble Us."

Here, the name used for "God" in the Hebrew is Elohim, a plural noun. Note the plural pronouns "We" and "Us." This again demonstrates not only the Chinese, but also the Hebrew concept of God—three divine Persons working as one, called the "Godhead" or the "Trinity" (p. 17).

great, noble, adult

So *God, Heaven* 天 , 人 （天） created a *great, noble, adult* 人 （大） man in His own image. God laid a *foundation* 氏 （氐） for humans in this first man, whom He called Adam.

foundation

The divine *Person* 𣥂 (人) made man in His own glorious, holy image ◇ , represented by a flame (see *God* 𣥺 p. 16). We clearly see the holy flame ◇ in the character *fire* 𣥻 [2] (火). Earth's first man had God's perfect, sinless character.

fire

$$ 𣥂 \quad + \quad ◇ \quad = \quad 𣥼 $$

Person   *flame, "holy"*   *foundation*

God named earth's first man "Adam" meaning "ground, earth" and also "red" in the Hebrew. We read further from their Scripture regarding Adam's creation:

> And the Lord God formed man of the dust of the ground, and breathed into his nostrils the breath of life; and man became a living being.[3]

earth, clay, dust

Note how the Chinese writing once more agrees with the Hebrew narrative. The radical *soil, earth* Ǭ [4] (土) shows God's holy attributes ◇ being transferred to the man of *clay* Ǭ (土) that He was forming from the dust of the ground — .

$$ ◇ \quad + \quad — \quad = \quad Ǭ $$

flame, "holy"   *ground*   *earth, soil (Adam)*

God formed a *complete* | (十) person (see | , p. 17) from the ground — , today designated as a *scholar* 士 [5] (土). The Early Zhou meaning of 士 is a "mature male person."

mature male person, scholar

$$ | \quad + \quad — \quad = \quad 士 $$

complete (person)   *ground*   *mature male person*

24

In the graph *holy* 〔graphic〕 [6] (聖) God's *hands* 〔graphic〕 are imparting His glorious character ◇ to the man of *clay* 〔graphic〕 which He was forming.

How appropriate the Hebrew Scriptures:

> Yet, O Lord, You are our Father. We are the clay. You are the potter; we are all the work of your hand.[7]

〔graphic〕 + 〔graphic〕 = 〔graphic〕

hands (God's)   *earth, clay*   *holy*

Several additional characters depict the creation of Adam from the dust of the earth. The graph 〔graphic〕 [8] (立) pictures a *noble* 〔graphic〕 (大) man standing on the ground — . This character has a number of significant meanings: *to stand, establish, found, create, start*—all of which, in displaying Adam coming up out of the ground, represent the original *creation* of humanity, the *founding, establishing, starting* of the human race.

〔graphic〕 + — = 〔graphic〕

noble, great   *"ground"*   *create, establish, found*

Yet another character depicting the first man arising from the dust of the earth is 〔graphic〕 [9] (壬), indicating *great, good*. Observe that the man 〔graphic〕 arises from the *earth, soil* 〔graphic〕 (土). On this sixth day of the creation week, according to the Hebrew Scriptures, "God saw everything that He had made, and indeed it was *very good.*"[10]

〔graphic〕 + 〔graphic〕 = 〔graphic〕

man (Adam)   *earth, clay*   *great, good*

〔graphic〕
holy

〔graphic〕
"hands of God"

〔graphic〕
create, found, start, establish, stand

〔graphic〕
great, good

The graph $\perp$ [11]($工$) meaning *work, artisan* pictures God ($\top$, p. 18) as an "artisan" creating the *mature male person* $\perp$ ($土$), Adam.

$\top$	+	$\perp$	=	$\underline{\underline{\mathrm{I}}}$
God		*mature maleperson*		*work, artisan*

It would seem that the Chinese considered God $\top$ as a *Worker of magic* H [12] ($巫$) in His creative activity. In H we find the Godhead (Trinity) portrayed as $\vdash\top\dashv$(compare with $\overline{\overline{\pi\pi}}$, p. 18), working together to form the *mature male person* $\perp$ ($土$), Adam.

To be created in the image of God meant Adam was perfect and sinless, even as ShangDi is perfect. ShangDi's dazzling perfection is spoken of as His "glory," which is represented as a fiery or sun-like appearance.

> O Lord my God, You are very great: You are clothed with honor and majesty, Who cover Yourself with light as with a garment.[13]

Therefore Adam, the first man, was originally clothed in a glorious, shining light, even as God. Before Adam sinned and disobeyed God, the Chinese characters portray his body as being covered with a glorious light, as having a fiery appearance. The character *naked, red* [14]($赤$) shows a *noble* $\bigwedge$ ($大$) man and a *fire* $\bigvee$ [15] ($火$). Adam was naked, but was clothed with a glorious "robe" pictured as fiery, possibly red-tinged. Since the Hebrew name "Adam" means not only "ground," but also "red," it may have been this imagery of a fiery covering that made both the Chinese and the Hebrews describe him as being red.

26

Margin labels:

$\underline{\underline{\mathrm{I}}}$ *work, artisan*

H *Worker of magic*

 naked, red

> You have made them [humans] a little lower than God, and crowned them with *glory a*nd honor.[16]

kneeling man

$$\text{大} \quad + \quad \text{火} \quad = \quad \text{赤}$$

noble (Adam)   *fire*   *naked, red*

A frequently seen graph in the oracle bone writing that shows a kneeling man 卩 [17](卩) must have original reference to Adam.

God *sealed, imprinted* [18] (印) His own image and character upon the man 卩 Adam when, with His *hand* [19] (手), He created him.

imprint

$$\text{卩} \quad + \quad \text{手} \quad = \quad \text{印}$$

kneeling man (Adam)   *hand (God's)*   *imprint*

When God created Adam, He placed him in a beautiful *large, wide, garden* 田 [20] (甫) called Eden. From the Hebrew we read:

> Now a river went out of Eden to water the garden, and from there it parted and became four riverheads.[21]

large, wide, garden, Father, beginning

If we look carefully at the graph 田 (甫), we can see the river originating in the center of the garden 田 and flowing in four directions 十 .

We promised earlier to identify the symbol Y as God (Y , p. 21). So, as we examine the character 田 (甫), meaning *garden, beginning, Father,* we find the Father-God Y arising from the garden's center 田 . *Field* 田 [22](田) also represents the garden of Eden and is a frequently-found character.

garden, field

All during that sixth day of the creation week, Adam was given the task of naming the animals as God formed them.

> So He [God] took some soil from the ground and formed all the animals and all the birds. Then He brought them to the man to see what he would name them;. . .but not one of them was a suitable companion to help him.[23]

It was not ShangDi's intention to leave Adam without a mate. So as this first momentous sixth day was drawing to a close, we read again from the Hebrew writings:

> Then the Lord God said, "It is not good that man should be alone; I will make him a helper comparable to him."[24]

Was Adam's companion to be made of the soil as he had been? No, this was not God's beautiful and meaningful purpose. Adam would appreciate his wife even more when he learned ShangDi's unique plan for the creation of woman! We learn from the Hebrew record:

woman

> Then the Lord God made the man fall into a deep sleep, and while he was sleeping, he took out one of the man's ribs and closed up the flesh. He formed a woman out of the rib and brought her to him.[25]

suitable, to prepare

With His *hand* 𝄞 (手), God *prepared* 𝄢 [26] (妥) a *suitable* wife for Adam, a *woman* 𝄫 [27] (女).

$$𝄞 \quad + \quad 𝄫 \quad = \quad 𝄢$$

| hand (God's) | woman | suitable, prepare |

ShangDi conducted the first marriage ceremony, as the Hebrew text describes it:

For this reason a man. . . [is] *united* to his wife, and they will become one flesh.[28]

to unite, join

The character *to unite, join* [29] (竝) pictures the first couple, hand in hand, joined in marriage.

God announced to them,

"Be fruitful and multiply, and fill the earth and sudue it; and have dominion. . . over every living thing that moves upon the earth."[30]

light, glorious, naked

One additional text from the Hebrew script should be quoted at this point:

The man and the woman were both *naked*, but they were not ashamed.[31]

fire

There was a reason why they were not ashamed to appear naked before God. They had been made in God's image (see *naked* ⚇ p.26). An additional frequently-used character meaning both *light, glorious* and *naked* 光 , 光 [32](光), also pictures both the man ⅄ and the *woman* 光 , although naked, covered with *a fiery* ⩗ , ⩗ [33] (火) robe .

roof, house

⅄ , 光 + ⩗, ⩗ = 光 , 光

man, woman   *fire*   *naked, glorious, light*

palace

What was the home that God prepared for Adam and Eve like? According to the ancient Chinese, it was a *palace* 宮 [34] 宮 [35](宮). Under the *roof* ⌂ [36](宀) are two *adult persons* □ + □ [37] (丁) cleverly united as 宮 .

⌂ + □ □ = 宮

house, roof   *two adult persons*   *palace*

□
adult person

29

The *home* ⌒ (⌒) of the first couple was to have God
⊤ (示) in its center. They would *follow, honor*  [38]
(宗) God's *religion* .

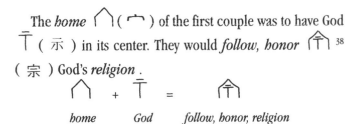

home   God   follow, honor, religion

The numeral *six* ⌒[39](六) depicts a home, for it was on
the sixth day of the creation week that the first home was established. It seems that the Chinese may have originally had
the same knowledge as the Hebrews, that God created everything in six days. The creation of these first two humans completed the earth and its furnishings. We read from the Hebrew:

> Thus the heavens and the earth were completed in all
> their vast array. By the *seventh* day God had finished
> the work He had been doing; so on the *seventh* day
> He *rested* from all His work. And God blessed the
> seventh day and made it holy, because on it He rested
> from all the work of creating that He had done.[40]

Not only had God rested on the seventh day from His great
creative works, but He commanded man to also rest on this
day. *To rest in* [41] (宅) depicts a house ⌒ where, on
the *seventh* ⊤ [42] (七) day its occupants were to rest.

⌒ + ⊤ = 宅

house   seven   to rest in

Thus the weekly cycle of seven days was established at creation and has been kept ever since, worldwide. The week is
not regulated by the movement of the earth, sun, moon, or
stars, but reflects only the great historic work of the Creator,
ShangDi.

30

*follow,
honor,
religion*

six

to rest in

seven

5

Secrets of a Lost Garden

Just what kind of an environment did ShangDi provide for our first parents? From the Hebrew Scripture, we read a description.

> And the Lord God planted a garden in Eden, in the
> east; and there He put the man whom He had formed.
> And out of the ground the Lord God made to grow
> every tree that is pleasant to the sight and good for
> food, the tree of life also in the midst of the garden,
> and the tree of the knowledge of good and evil.
>
> A river flowed out of Eden to water the garden, and
> there it divided and became four rivers.[1]

field,
"garden"

This garden paradise has actually been illustrated with drawings in the Chinese calligraphy. We have already discussed the much-used graph *field* ⊞ [2](⊞ , p. 27), that would seem to have reference specifically to this first lovely Garden of Eden.

to walk,
travel, path

to overflow,
spread out

river

Note also the phonetic similarity (pronounced "dien" in the early Zhou dynasty)[3] to "Eden" in the Hebrew ("ay-den").[4]

At first glance, ⊞ (田) appears to be a well-irrigated field, but in light of the Hebrew description that there was a river which divided into four rivers flowing out of Eden to water the garden, we may have another concept. According to this pictograph, the river originated in the very center, with streams flowing in four directions (⊕, p. 27). To give a force of flow to the rivers, its source must have been elevated, on a mountain.

To walk, travel, a path ⌐ [5] (行) may well have originally depicted the bifurcation of the four rivers on the central area of the *mountain* ⋈ [6] (山). Of this we can be sure by examining [7](衍), meaning *to overflow, spread out*, describing the *rivers* [8](川) as they spread out in four directions ⊕ . This would suggest that Adam and Eve traveled to this place.

$$ \text{(to walk)} \quad + \quad \text{(river)} \quad = \quad \text{(to overflow)} $$

to walk　　*river*　　*to overflow*

Let us re-examine the character with multiple meanings, *garden, beginning, Father* 甫 (甫 , p. 27), for in it we find God Ψ in the very center of the garden as 甫 . The holy *mountain* ⋈ (山) of Eden appears to have been the site where God met with Adam and Eve who had *traveled* ⌐ (行) there. Their destination would have been the *region* [9](州) , on God's holy mountain, depicted as a "holy" ◇ (pp. 24, 25) place surrounded by water — perhaps on the central peak of God's holy mountain.

mountain

region

32

The character *spring, fountain* 𣱳 10 (泉), gives additional insight, revealing the wellspring of the four-headed river. Most rivers originate from converging streams high in the mountains. This graph 𣱳 portrays the actual source of the living waters ⁝⟨⟩⁝ 11 (水) is God 丅 (p. 17), with waters ⁝⟨⟩⁝ shown flowing from Him, the true "fountain of life."

spring, source,
fountain

Another important feature of the garden were two special trees.

> And out of the ground the Lord God made every tree grow that is pleasant to the sight and good for food. The *tree of life* was also in the midst of the garden, and the *tree of the knowledge of good and evil.*12

These two important *trees* 朮朮 13 (林), therefore, must have been located on the holy mountain in the center of the garden.

"God
radical"

We will find that there are many oracle bone forms for *mountain* ⛰ ,6 ⛰, ⛰, ⛰14 (山), but surprisingly these very same characters are also used for *fire* (火)! From this we can assume that God's glorious, holy presence, as a fire, enshrouded His holy mountain.

water

For example, examine the character *burning* 朮朮 15 (焚). We find there the *mountain* ⛰ (山), but the symbol ⛰ also indicates *fire*. Furthermore, on the mountain are the two special *trees* 朮朮 (林), the tree of life and the tree of the knowledge of good and evil.

trees

⛰   +   朮朮   =   朮朮⛰

mountain, fire   *trees*   *burning*

burning

center, place, moral pattern

to walk with, be near to, depend on

We have already specified that the spring was symbolic of God and was the source of the four-headed river of life that originated from the center of the garden. The graphs meaning *center, place, moral pattern* 㞷, 屮 [16] (方), provide most interesting information. In 㞷 we find a *Person* 𠂊 (人) with attributes of God (丅丅, see p. 26): our *moral pattern*. Next examine 㞷 [17] (傍) meaning *to walk along side of, to be near to, to depend on*. Adam and Eve could freely visit God on the holy mountain in Eden's center. They *walked* with Him and were *dependent on* Him.

$$屮 \quad + \quad 行 \quad = \quad 傍$$

moral pattern (God)   *to travel*   *to depend on, be near*

Now listen to what the Hebrew text tells us about God's mountain, the river, the spring (fountain), and the people:

> Thy righteousness is like the mountains of God,…
> How precious is Thy steadfast love, O God!
> The children of men take refuge in the shadow of Thy wings.
> They *feast* on the abundance of Thy house,
> and Thou givest them drink from the *river* of Thy delights.
> For with Thee is the *fountain* of life.[18]

Again, both the Chinese characters and the Hebrew Scripture portray several identical features of the first garden home:

1. A four-headed river flows from the *garden* 田 and waters it.

2. The source of the river is a *spring* 㡛 in the *center* 㐅 of the garden.

3. The *spring* 㡛 is symbolic of *God* 〒 as the "Fountain of life."

4. The *garden* ⊞ encompasses God's *mountain* 𖽄 , His "house" or earthly dwelling place.

5. The first couple, "the children of men," come to commune with and *to be near to* 㐄 God . (This includes feasting—apparently on fruit from the tree of life—and drinking from the river of life. Eating and drinking from these two sources assured Adam and Eve of immortality, for this is why the tree of life and the river of life were so named.)

God had invited Adam and Eve to pick and eat the fruit from the tree of life, so they returned there frequently. On the other hand, God had a specific warning for Adam initially, and later for Eve:

> And the Lord God commanded the man, saying, "Of every tree of the garden you may freely eat; but of the tree of the knowledge of good and evil you shall not eat, for in the day that you eat of it you shall surely die."[19]

Is there a pictograph portraying the tree of life—so called because eating of its fruit gave immortality? It would seem that 㮮 [20] (栗) meaning *rich and full, awe-inspiring*, fits this magnificent , *fiery* ꙮꙮ (火 , p. 24)) tree. These three *fires* ꙮ (火) represent the fiery glory of the Trinity (see ⁀ p. 19), for the Hebrew Scriptures say, "Our God is a consum-

*rich and full,
awe-inspiring*

ing *fire.*"[21] (Note again the flame ◊ in *fire* ∨∨). God provided *rich and full,* everlasting life as Adam and Eve ate from this tree.

ᵛᵛ∨ + 𝕏 = 🌲

fiery   *tree*   *rich and full, awe-inspiring*

The character 𝕏 [22](休) to rest, be happy, pictures a 𝄐 person resting and enjoying the tree 𝕏 of life.

𝄐 + 𝕏 = 𝕏

person   *tree*   *to rest, be happy*

Might there also be a graph representing the tree of the knowledge of good and evil? The character currently meaning *mulberry tree* 🌳 [23] (桑) which has reaching *hands* 𝜓𝜓 for branches, would appear to describe this tree. Note that two *mouths* ∪ + ∪ (口), indicating eating, are found at this tree in the character *to die, lose, ruin, perish* 🌳 [24] (喪). One more evidence that 🌳 is the forbidden tree is that 🌳 and 🌳 are phonetically identical ("sang"), except for tone.

𝜓𝜓 + 𝕏 = 🌳 + ∪∪ = 🌳

hands   *tree*   *mulberry tree*   *mouths*   *to die, perish*

The ancient Chinese give us several picture-words of the first couple in their garden home. First, we'll analyze the character *male, feudal title* 田丿 [25] (男). The *garden* 田 is recognized. The second radical, *power, strength* ⼂ , ⼃ [26] (力), needs some amplification. ⼂ is a pictogram of an arm and hand, in fact, God's *right* arm. Note this text from the Hebrews:

to rest, be happy

mulberry tree

to die, lose, ruin, perish

male, feudal title

⼂ ⼃

power, strength

> With My great *power* and *outstretched arm*
> I made the earth and its people and the animals that
> are on it, and I give it to anyone I please.[27]

Apparently, God is giving the garden of Eden to Adam, the *noble* 大 (大) man, receiver of this feudal title, also the first male. Adam received his land, the garden ⊞ from the hand of the King, God.

$$power, strength \quad + \quad garden \quad = \quad male, feudal\ title$$

Additional support that 𠃌 is indeed God's arm (and not man's) can be found in the character 劦 [28] (劦) indicating *united in accord*.

$$power\ (of\ Trinity) \quad + \quad mouth \quad = \quad united\ in\ accord$$

united in accord

This graph represents the dual creative might of the Godhead: three *strong* 劦 arms of the Trinity, and the *power* of God's spoken 口 word.

An alternate writing for this character is 劦 [29] (劦), definitely showing God's 丁 *power* 丿 in speech 口 .

> For He *spoke*, and it was done;
> He *commanded* and it stood fast.[30]

Now it was God's plan to make Adam the *field supervisor* 畯 [31] (畯) of Eden, as this pictogram shows. We recognize the *garden* ⊞ , and Adam 𠂉 (see p. 27), the field supervisor.

field supervisor

Then the Lord God took the man and put him
in the garden of Eden to tend and keep it.[32]

$$\text{𝄐} \quad + \quad \boxplus \quad = \quad \text{田}$$

kneeling man (Adam)   *garden*   *field supervisor*

How delighted Adam and Eve must have been with their
beautiful surroundings in the garden of Eden! Their loving Father-God ShangDi had provided everything for their comfort
and benefit. On every hand were luscious fruit-bearing trees.
Many-colored gorgeous flowers surrounded them. In the center of the garden, four sparkling rivers streamed from the sides
of a magnificent mountain, God's earthly dwelling place.

*to rest, stop,
settle*

Eden's special mountain, which was visited by ShangDi,
becomes more intriguing as we consider additional characters related to it. In the Hebrew Scripture, God's place of *rest*
[33] (止), or dwelling place, is called the "hill of the Lord"
or "His holy place." *Rest, to stop, settle* (止)is actually a
pictograph of a foot.

descend

mount

We can understand from the character *to descend* [34]
(降) that it is God who is descending from heaven to *rest,*
with feet pointed downward , on His holy *mount* ,
 [35](阝).

cliff

$$\text{𝄐} \quad + \quad \text{𝄐} \quad = \quad \text{𝄐}$$

mount   *feet*   *descend*

By turning *mountain* (山) on its side, we find the
character *mount* , [35](阝). The second symbol

may be explained by stacking the character *cliff* ┌ 36 (厂)
three deep as 𠃊 .

We can erase the last doubt that the Garden of Eden had a
holy *hill* 𨺉 37 (陵)when we analyze this character. The
mount ⻏ (⻏) is identified, as well as a *noble* 大 person.

The *noble* 大 person *stopping at* 𦣻 (止) that place
could again represent either Adam or Eve coming to the holy
hill to worship God.

hill

$$ 大 \quad + \quad 𦣻 \quad + \quad ⻏ \quad = \quad 𨺉 $$

noble (person)   stop   mount   hill

Let us make one more relevant comparison with the Hebrew record, which reads:

> Who shall ascend the hill of the Lord?
> And who shall stand in His holy place?
> He who has clean hands and a pure heart,
> who does not lift up his soul to what is false,
> and does not swear deceitfully.
> He will receive blessing from the Lord.[38]

As long as Adam and Eve remained "pure in heart" and
sinless, they could worship at God's holy hill. That the *cliff*
┌ (厂) also represented the holy hill is apparent from the
next character. With joy, Adam and Eve could meet God 丫
on the holy mount ┌ and hear the *sound* of His *voice*
𦕔 39 (聲) with the *ear* 耳 40 (耳).

sound,
voice

ear

have an
audience
with, meet

eye

$$ 丫 \quad + \quad ┌ \quad + \quad 耳 \quad = \quad 𦕔 $$

God   cliff (mount)   ear   sound, voice

Adam 𠂤 (儿), with Eve, was able *to have an audience,
meet* 𝕏 41 (見) *eye to eye* 𝕏 42 (目) with God.

$$𠂤 \quad + \quad 𝕏 \quad = \quad 𝕏$$

kneeling man (Adam)   *Eye*   *meet*

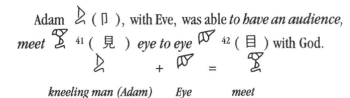

*watch over,
observe*

This face-to-face communion with God was a wonderful
privilege. God always *watched over* and *observed* 𝕏 43
(省) Adam and Eve as their Protector.

$$Y \quad + \quad 𝕏 \quad = \quad 𝕏$$

God   *eye*   *watch over, observe*

But, sadly, this meeting together with God would not always
be theirs to enjoy. We will learn the reason for their estrange-
ment from ShangDi, their Creator-God and benefactor, as we
continue our study.

6

Invader in the Garden

There is no doubt that originally a tender relationship existed between ShangDi and the first couple! In the character *to be near to, follow closely* 𡘋 [1] (夾), this close relationship is quite obvious, for we recognize God, as a great, noble Being, with arms outstretched 大 , followed closely by two *persons* 人 + 人 (Adam and Eve) .

Sad events took place, however, that destroyed these ties, and separated Adam and Eve from their kind and beneficent Creator. In their many talks together, ShangDi had instructed Adam and Eve concerning an enemy, a mighty angel called Lucifer. This angel had rebelled against God's fair government of love in heaven.

Scenes of what took place regarding Lucifer in heaven are recorded by inspiration in the Hebrew Scriptures:

This is what the Sovereign Lord says:

*be near to,
follow closely*

"You [Lucifer] were the model of perfection,
   full of wisdom and perfect in beauty.
You were in Eden,
   the garden of God [in heaven]. ...
You were blameless in your ways
   from the day you were created
   till wickedness was found in you. ...

So I drove you in disgrace from the mount of God,
   and I expelled you, O guardian cherub,
   from among the fiery stones.
Your heart became proud
   on account of your beauty,
and you corrupted your wisdom
because of your splendor.
So I threw you to the earth."[2]

Again, we learn more of Lucifer, the morning star, from the Hebrew Scriptures:

How you have fallen from heaven,
   O morning star, son of the dawn!
You have been cast down to the earth....
You said in your heart,
   "I will ascend to heaven;
I will raise my throne
   above the stars of God;
I will sit enthroned on the mount of assembly,
   on the utmost heights of the sacred mountain.
I will ascend above the tops of the clouds;
   I will make myself like the Most High."[3]

Lucifer was not satisfied with his highest position among the angels. He wanted to be a god himself. So he inspired a mass discontent among the angels of heaven. As a result, one-third of the angels of heaven joined Lucifer (also called Satan and the devil) in this rebellion. We turn once again to the record of the Hebrew people:

> Now war arose in heaven, Michael and his angels fighting against the dragon; and the dragon and his angels fought, but they were defeated and there was no longer any place for them in heaven. And the great dragon was thrown down, that ancient serpent, who is called the Devil and Satan, the deceiver of the whole world—he was thrown down to the earth, and his angels were thrown down with him.[4]

There was no doubt that Lucifer would try to either destroy Adam and Eve or gain them as his allies in his great controversy with ShangDi. We should note in the above Hebrew narratives that "heaven," where God's throne is located on His sacred mountain, is also metaphorically called "the Garden of Eden." Thus we learn that the Garden of Eden which God prepared for Adam and Eve in the newly created earth was actually a miniature of heaven itself. So we should not be surprised that the earthly Eden also had a holy mountain.

As ShangDi talked daily with Adam and Eve on His holy mountain in the earthly Garden of Eden, He invited them to pick and eat freely of the tree of life 栗 (栗 , p. 35), for it would give them immortality—everlasting life.

rich and full, awe- inspiring

On the other hand, He had forbidden access to the other nearby tree in the middle of the garden, the tree of the knowledge of good and evil. Fruit from this tree was not theirs to eat—or even to touch, lest they die. We found this tree best

43

*to die, perish,
lose, ruin*

symbolized by (喪 , p. 35) *to die, perish.* God had imposed this one small, but important, test upon them to prove their loyalty to Him as their Creator and Benefactor.

Even before Eve was created on the sixth day of the first week, God had cautioned Adam,

> "You are free to eat from any tree in the garden; but you must not eat from the tree of the knowledge of good and evil, for when you eat of it you will surely die."[5]

Eve, of course, learned of the limitation later, for it applied to both of them.

*restrain,
bind*

The character, *to restrain, bind* [6] (束), gives details regarding God's command. In we find a *mouth* 凵 (口) superimposed on a *tree* 木 . The tree symbol slashing through the mouth radical suggests God's command, "Don't eat; *restrain* yourself!" Eating of this tree would bring them into bondage to Satan and sin.

$$凵 \quad + \quad 木 \quad = \quad 束$$

mouth (eating)   *tree*   *restrain*

God's word and instruction, however lovingly given, were no less than an *imperial decree* [7] (旨). The great *Being* 𠆢 , the Ruler of the universe, *speaks* 凵 (口). And it was a death decree, should they fail to prove loyal to His kingdom of love.

imperial decree

$$𠆢 \quad + \quad 凵 \quad = \quad 旨$$

Person (God)   *mouth*   *imperial decree*

Furthermore, this *command, mandate* 𝈪 [8] (令) was given by the *mouth* △ (inverted ⊔) of God to the kneeling man 𝈪 , Adam.

𝈪   +   △   =   𝈪

kneeling man (Adam)   *mouth (God's)*   *command*

command, mandate

One day, when Eve had become separated from her husband, she passed through the center of the garden. Suddenly she heard an unfamiliar voice. It was not Adam or ShangDi speaking. Who could it be? The voice seemed to come from the tree of the knowledge of good and evil. She stopped, intrigued and curious. Eve stood at the *tree* 木 of the knowledge of good and evil. There, sure enough, was a beautiful serpent—and it was he who was talking!

The talking serpent was a *foreigner* 夷 [9] (夷) whose intent was to *exterminate, kill* the *noble* 大 person (Adam or Eve). Note the serpentlike individual 𢀖 [10] (夷) which looms as a threat to the *noble* 大 person. We can know it is the serpent who does the killing because *kill* (夷) is also written with the serpent-man alone as 𢀖 .

𢀖   +   大   =   夷

"serpent"   *noble (person, Eve)*   *foreigner, to kill*

foreigner, kill, exterminate

The foreigner, disguised as a serpent, addressed the unsuspecting Eve. This graph 𢀖 [10] has also been transcribed as (尸), meaning a *representative of the dead*— an accurate indentity for Satan, that "old serpent." Satan, for in his rebellion against God, he had cut himself off from God, the source

representative of the dead

of all life. He was spiritually dead, eventually to become the instigator and representative of all those who rebel against God.

The devil had waited for just this opportunity to approach Eve when she was alone. It was his plan to tempt her privately with his persuasive argument. The serpent began a conversation by asking, "Did God really tell you not to eat fruit from any tree in the garden?"[11]

negative, no, not

Eve answered, showing that she understood exactly the restrictions God had made:

> "We may eat the fruit of any tree in the garden ... except the tree in the middle of it. God told us not to eat the fruit of that tree or even touch it; if we do, we will die."[12]

But the devil scoffingly answered, "You will not surely die."[13] By this statement, the devil was completely negating what God had said. How interesting that one oracle bone character for *negative, no, not* 林[14] (弗) depicts the serpent 弓 in the forbidden *tree* 木, which stood next to the *tree* 木 of life. A more common oracle bone writing is written simply as 坤 .

$$ 弓 \quad + \quad 林 \quad = \quad 林 $$

serpent   *trees*   *negative, no, not*

In his conversation with Eve, the devil continued:

> "For God knows that when you eat of it [the tree of the knowledge of good and evil] your eyes will be opened, and you will be like God, knowing good and evil."[15]

Unfortunately, Eve did not realize that the serpent was one to fear. Humanity's fate hung in the balance. Would Eve obey God or fall into the devil's snare?

46

7

The Fatal Bite

Follow with us the steps in the devil's deception of the woman who stood before the tree of the knowledge of good and evil. As she looked at the lovely tree, Eve was soon convinced that she need not fear death and that God was intentionally withholding good from them.

> The woman saw that the tree was good for food, that it was pleasant to the eyes, and a tree desirable to make one wise.[1]

She looked at the forbidden tree and saw that it was "pleasant to the eyes," with beautiful fruit. The fruit was *desirable* or *"covetable"* [2] (婪). In this character, we find the *woman* facing one *tree*, coveting the fruit, with her back to the second *tree*. These characters record that it was not Adam, but the *woman* who initially distrusted ShangDi and disregarded His warning.

desire, covet

woman   +   trees   =   desire, covet

The Hebrew Scripture reports, "She took of its fruit and ate."[3] Eve had been no match for the wily serpent. He was *strong, violent, compelling* 𢎛 [4] (弜). In this figure, we see a *person* 𠂉 , Eve, being molded by the *strong foreigner* 𢎁 (夷) into one like himself 𢎛 . Eve became like Lucifer!

strong, violent, compelling

$$𢎁 \quad + \quad 𠂉 \quad = \quad 𢎛$$

foreigner   person (Eve)   strong, compelling

She did not yet realize the consequence of her yielding to the suggestion of the devil, so she rushed to Adam with some of the fruit.

> And she also gave some to her husband, and he ate[5]

to die, perish

When Adam found that his lovely wife had disobeyed God's one command and eaten the forbidden fruit, what should he do? He quickly decided to join in Eve's disobedience and hurriedly ate the forbidden fruit. Again examine the character *to die, perish* 喪 (喪 , p. 36), and note the two *mouths* 𠮛𠮛 (口), indicating eating fruit from the forbidden *tree* 朮 .

disobedient

Both Adam and Eve had fallen into the devil's cleverly planned trap! They had become *disobedient* 屰 [6] (屰). Note the fallen, upside-down *noble* 大 man. Actually, they had *re-belled, acted contrary to* 逆 [7] (逆)God's specific instructions. The *disobedient* 屰 (屰) couple had *walked* 彳 (行) and *stopped* 止 (止) contrary to God's one mandate.

rebel, act contrary to

$$屰 \quad + \quad 彳 \quad + \quad 止 \quad = \quad 逆$$

disobedient   walked   stopped   rebel, contrary to

to walk

48

They had been tricked! They soon realized their understanding had not been broadened to their benefit, but to their great loss.

> Then the eyes of both were opened, and
> they knew that they were naked.[8]

As the glorious light signifying their sinless perfection and resemblance to God began fading, they discovered their nakedness. Hastily "they sewed fig leaves together and covered themselves."[9] Ashamed and naked, knowing ShangTi would soon be visiting them, they quickly made clothes of fig leaves. *Clothes* [10] (衣) is a simple radical in which we find Adam, a *person* ╲ , and Eve, a second *person* ╱ . (Eve's origin from Adam's side ╳ is pictured.) The couple ╳ needed something *to cover, over* ⌒╲ (亠) them. In a matter of a few minutes, Lucifer had accomplished his goal of separating the human family from ShangDi. The devil substituted distrust and suspicion for loyalty and love to the heavenly Parent.

clothes

By their *disobedient* ￥ (弟) act of intentionally eating the fruit from the forbidden *tree* 朮 , they would forfeit access to the fruit from the tree of life which provided immortality as long as they regularly ate from it. God's plan had been that they eat daily of the tree of life and live forever.

The time for ShangDi's *descent from heaven* (降 , see p. 38) and daily visit had come. This interesting pictogram shows movement, for both of God's feet are depicted in contrast to a single foot, meaning *stop, rest* ∀ (p. 38). Also notice the downward direction of His feet , indicating His descent. God came down to His sacred *mount* ⴼ (阝) to

descent from heaven

49

meet with Adam and Eve. He, of course, already knew what had happened.

> That evening they heard the Lord God walking in the garden, and they hid from Him among the trees. But the Lord God called out to the man, "Where are you?"[11]

So Adam and Eve stood before their Creator, who looked at their hastily-put-together, fig-leaf garments and asked, "Did you eat the fruit that I told you not to eat?"[12]

ShangDi knew the *couple* 𠆢 + 𠆢 had made a fatal *stop* 止 (止) in the *garden* 甫 (甫 , pp.27, 32). They had *stumbled, slipped* and *fallen* 壹 [13] (壹) into the first sin through the devil's snare.

𠆢 + 𠆢 + 止 + 甫 = 壹

persons (two)   stop   garden   stumble, fall

There followed a series of accusations and excuses with first Adam, then Eve making their alibis:

> The man answered, "The woman you put here with me gave me the fruit, and I ate it." ...
> She replied, "The snake tricked me into eating it."[14]

God spoke first to Lucifer His enemy, who henceforth became known as Satan, "the old serpent," "the devil," and the "dragon":

> "I will put enmity [hatred]
> Between you and the woman,
> And between your seed and her Seed;
> He shall bruise your head,
> And you shall bruise His heel."[15]

stumble, slip, fall

garden

Examine the character *snake* 它 [16] (蛇) which graphically portrays this very statement: *foot* 止 (止) stepping on 它 , a symbol representing the serpent.

snake

$$ 止 + 它 = 它 $$

| foot | serpent | snake |

In this curse put upon His foe, ShangDi pronounced, for the first time, a wonderful plan for humanity's ultimate salvation. Through later descendants of the woman Eve, would eventually come the Savior, the promised Seed. In the character meaning *good* 好 [17] (好), we find the *Seed, offspring, Son* 子 [18] (子) of the *woman* 女 (女).

seed, son
offspring

$$ 子 + 女 = 好 $$

| Seed, Son | woman | good |

good

It would seem that the ancient Chinese recognized a special, holy Seed, one who would crush and utterly defeat the devil and his angels. But in so doing, the Savior would suffer great agony on behalf of the guilty human race. This Savior was one of the Godhead, God the "Son," who would one day come as a human being to earth.

death

But the ultimate death 死 [19] (死) of the devil, who had intruded into the garden was also assured. Let us look closely at the graph 歹 which would appear to have originally represented God Fon the holy mount. The symbol 卜 [20] (卜) means *to foretell*, and in 歹 [21] (歹) indicating *bad, wicked*, pictures God on the mount in prophetic judgment of wicked persons. In 死 , He is pronouncing the death sentence on

to foretell

bad, wicked

51

the serpent, the father of lies. Compare 𠂤 with 𠂤 (p. 39).
Both have God ⌐ , ⅄ on the mount (p. 38).

$$ 𠂤 \quad + \quad 〉 \quad = \quad 𠂤〉 $$

bad   *"serpent"*   *death*

Next, ShangDi addressed Eve:

> "I will greatly multiply
> your sorrow and your conception;
> In pain you shall bring forth children;
> Your desire shall be for your husband,
> And he shall rule over you."[22]

Doubtless, God had originally intended the bearing of children to be a completely joyful experience. However, the bodily deterioration that womankind would suffer as the result of sin would no longer permit this. Pain and *difficulty* [23] (困) would become the lot of women in childbirth. From this time also, the husband would rule over the wife. She would fall from her original position as his equal. All of this *difficulty* had resulted from eating fruit from the forbidden *tree* 木 in the garden *enclosure* ☐ .

difficulty, trouble

$$ 木 + \quad ☐ \quad = \quad 困 $$

tree   *(garden) enclosure*   *difficulty, trouble*

And what of Adam? His sorrow was also specific. Said God:

> "Cursed is the ground because of you;
> through painful toil you will eat of it
> all the days of your life.
> Both *thorns* and thistles
> it shall bring forth for you,
> And you shall eat the herb of the field.
> By the sweat of your brow

> you will eat your food
> until you return to the ground,
> > since from it you were taken;
> for dust you are
> > and to dust you will return."[24]

thorns

From the character *thorns* [25] (楚), we see that the result of a *person* □ [26] (丁) making a *stop* ∀ (止) in the middle of the garden at the special trees 林 was a curse upon the ground. Adam would henceforth encounter *thorns*.

□ + 林 = (thorns glyph)

person	*trees*	*thorns*

One must understand that the moment Eve stopped and ate of the forbidden tree was the beginning of man's succeeding history of decline. The graph [27] (歷) meaning *in due course, subsequently, a series of,* defines the cause: the *stopping* ∀ (止) to eat of the forbidden *tree* 木 . This then precipitated *in due course, the subsequent series* (glyph) (歷) of man's decline ever since that fatal stop.

in due course, subsequent series

∀ + 林 = (in due course glyph)

stop	*trees*	*in due course, subsequent series*

Now all Adam could do was *mourn* [28] (弔) that he, *man* 人 , had become entangled with the serpent ∫ .

mourn

人 + ∫ = (mourn glyph)

person (Adam)	*serpent*	*mourn*

ShangDi had pronounced upon humanity the sure penalty of death for disobedience. An inscription, *in consequence of, because, reason* [29] (囚), depicts a *noble* 人 man in the garden *enclosure* □ .

because, reason, in consequence of, death

53

Adam was that man, condemned to death because of disobedience. The character 因 has also been transcribed as *death* (死).

The fact that Adam and Eve lived on after their disobedience indicates that their death was ultimate and that they no longer possessed immortality.

Sin had now separated our first parents from their sinless God. They could no longer meet face-to-face. Because of Adam's disobedience, God had declared, "For dust you are, and to dust you shall return."[31] Eve must suffer the same fate.

How true the familiar Chinese saying: *"In the beginning, man's original character was virtuous"*: 人之初 性本善. Unfortunately, humanity's perfect, sinless character was lost by a single willful act. Adam and Eve had eaten the forbidden fruit, knowing full well that they were disobeying the expressed command of their loving, kind Creator. They had listened to the words of the devil rather than to God's warning.

Adam and Eve's alienation from the Life-Giver meant death, an inescapable consequence. They had forfeited immortality for not only themselves, but for all their posterity. And they had brought all this not only upon themselves but upon us as well.

8

A Costly Rescue Plan

Sorrowfully, God must now expel His beloved Adam and Eve from the Garden of Eden. The Hebrew record next states:

And the Lord God said, "The man has now become like one of us, knowing good and evil. He must not be allowed to reach out his hand and take also from the tree of life and eat, and live forever." So the Lord God banished him from the Garden of Eden to work the ground from which he had been taken. After he drove the man out, he placed on the east side of the Garden of Eden cherubim [angels] and a flaming sword flashing back and forth to guard the way to the tree of life.[1]

Interestingly, one of the ancient books of the Zhou dynasty, records: "Because man sinned in ancient times, the God of heaven [天帝] ordered Chung and Li to block up the way between heaven and earth."[2] Perhaps Chung and Li were the names given by the Chinese to the two angels on either side of Eden's gate.

So God expelled Adam and Eve from the garden. As they

gate

passed through the eastern garden *gate* 門 3 (門), they realized this meant their exclusion from the life-giving tree of life and immortality. Note the hands 北 blocking the *gate* 門 entrance. They could not go past the gate to eat from the *tree* 木 of life. There were two angels (cherubim) guarding the way.

alone

Adam and Eve, now turned out of the garden, were *alone* 単 4 (單). The conjoined couple ◇◇ are depicted outside the *garden* 田 . The man 卩 (卩) and his wife, the *woman* 㠯 had become *aliens* 畏 , 畏 5 (鬼), having been expelled from the *garden* 田 .

卩 ,	㠯	+	田	=	畏 , 畏
man,	woman		garden		aliens

alien

Now they found themselves in *strange, different* 異 6 (異) surroundings, and they felt their need of communion with God. Depicted outside the *garden* 田 is a figure with upraised hands, a characteristic posture of worship.

大	+	田	=	異
worshiping figure		garden		strange, different

strange, different

Whereas Adam had previously loved to meet with God, now he was filled with *fear* and *dread* 畏 7 (畏). God is represented by the tall Person who *prophesies* 卜 (卜 , p. 51) the fate of Adam, the exiled *alien* 鬼 (鬼).

亻	+	田	=	鬼	+	卜	=	畏
person		garden		alien (Adam)		prophesy (God)		fear, dread

dread, fear,

The devil had claimed that God was withholding good from them. If at this point ShangDi had abandoned Adam and Eve

56

as hopeless rebels who could not even observe the smallest and simplest request possible, we might have to agree with the devil. But God did not leave His beloved Adam and Eve without hope. Already He had promised a Savior in the *Seed* 㝭 (子 , p. 51) of the woman. Now He wanted to explain more of the coming Savior's love for lost humanity.

Seed

ShangDi viewed the miserable fig leaf *clothes* ╱ (衣 , p. 49) Adam and Eve had fashioned for themselves. A costly and symbolic demonstration followed as the lives of innocent animals were sacrificed to provide skins to reclothe the sorrowing couple.

clothes

> The Lord God made garments of skin for Adam
> and his wife and clothed them.[8]

Never before had they witnessed the awfulness of death. Their beautiful animal friends were killed, thus symbolizing the death of God's sinless Son, One of the Godhead, who would one day come to earth as a human being and ultimately give His life for humanity.

This great act of clothing Adam and Eve with the skins of the sacrificial animals carries deep meaning and is memorialized in several Chinese characters. It was the *beginning* ╱[9] (初) of the plan of salvation for humanity. The symbolic *clothes* ╱ of skins for the guilty pair were provided only by the slaying of animals with a *knife* ╱ [10] (刀).

beginning

knife

╱ + ╱ = ╱

knife   clothes   beginning

The new *garments* 衣 (衣) were a gift from God . Again we find the united *persons* 人 (p. 49) who are symbolically *clothed* 衣 with the righteous character of the promised Son.

Another character also using the significant radical *clothes* 衣 is *to depend on, rely on* 依 [11] (依). Inserted into the graph is the great *Being* 人 , God, whose provision of *garments* 衣 of skin for the couple 人 was meant to teach Adam and Eve that they needed to *rely on* 依 Him for hope of salvation from eternal death.

to depend on, rely on

$$\land \ + \ 人 \ = \ 衣 \ + \ 人 \ = \ 依$$

cover   couple   clothes   Person(God)   depend, rely on

Innocent animals had *to die* 卒 [12] (卒) by Adam's *hand* 手 so that God could provide *clothes* 衣 for them. It is likely the creatures sacrificed were *sheep* 羊 [13] (羊), for this animal above all others was to symbolize God's own Son who was later to be called "the Lamb of God who takes away the sin of the world."[14]

to die

sheep

$$手 \ + \ 衣 \ = \ 卒$$

hand   clothes   to die

righteousness

In the character for *righteousness* 義 [15] (義), we find the *sheep* 羊 , like a garment, covering over *me* 我 [16] (我). But "me" is composed of a hand 手 and a weapon, a *lance* 弋 [17] (弋)—which tells the story that *I* am responsible for the death of the *Lamb*, for my hand 手 holds the killing instrument.

I, me

lance,

$$\text{⟏} + \text{丄} = \text{𡉏} + \text{⅄} = \text{𡉏}$$

hand   lance   me   sheep   righteousness

Originally, it was Adam and Eve whose sins were covered by the righteous *Lamb* ⅄ of God. We discover this in the character *beautiful* 𡘺 [18] (美), for the *noble* 𠆢, person(s), Adam or Eve is portrayed. When the Lamb covered their sins, they were indeed beautiful in God's eyes, for He could see only His sinless Son, symbolized by the *lamb* ⅄ . It was time for them to think, not about their punishment, but about God's love, goodness, and mercy, in spite of their ungrateful disloyalty.

beautiful

$$\text{𠆢} + \text{⅄} = \text{𡘺}$$

noble (person)   sheep   beautiful

The *gate* 門 (門 , p. 54) of Eden was evidently a place of glory, as indicated by the character *fiery* 閃 [19] (閃), where a *fire* ⋎ (火 , pp. 24, 35) is recognized.

gate

> [God] placed cherubim [angels] at the east of the garden of Eden, and a flaming sword which turned every way.[20]

fiery

$$\text{門} + \text{⋎} = \text{閃}$$

gate   fire   fiery, glorious

In another passage of Hebrew Scripture and at another time, God says, "I will speak with you … from between the two cherubim…."[21] Of God, the Scriptures also state, "Give ear, … You [God] who dwell between the cherubim, shine forth!"[22] Could not the flashing sword represent God's glorious presence there at Eden's gate?

fire

The garden *gate* 門 (門 , p. 54) was also the site where they came to *ask, inquire* 問 [23] (問) of God concerning their needs.

門 + 口 = 問

gate　　　　mouth　　　to ask, inquire

The *gate* 門 was the place they came to *listen, hear* 聞 [24] (聞) with the *ear* 耳 (耳 , p. 39) to what God had to say to them. This oracle bone writing of *listen, hear* shows the kneeling figure listening with the *ear* 耳 (耳). It is no coincidence that this appears to be a symbol of *fire* and *mountain* (火 , 山 , p. 33, 35) in a vertical position— which would intimate where Adam received his original instruction from God.

kneeling figure　　　ear　　　　to listen , hear

The character for *sacrifice* 祭 [25] (祭) has ancient roots. In this, we recognize the hand 手 with a vessel of *blood* 血 , [26] (血) serving God 示 (示 , p. 17).

hand　　　blood　　　God　　　sacrifice

Compare the abbreviated *blood* symbol with 主 [27] (主) meaning *Lord, Master, Ruler*. This appears to be a combination of *blood* and God 丫 , defining that the "Lord, Master" is God who will one day shed His blood for mankind.

blood　　　　God　　　　Lord, Master

The *blood* graph will be explained fully in Chapter 10.

Margin glossary (left column):

to ask, inquire

listen, hear

sacrifice

blood

Lord, Master, Ruler (God)

The sheep ⵣ (羊) was not the only animal used in the worship of ShangDi, for the *bullock, ox* ♀ ²⁸ (牛) was also offered. Note that the lower part of the graphs ⵣ , ♀ , and ♀ , share the same God ⵣ symbol (see p. 27). Furthermore, the sacrificial animals must be unblemished, or perfect. Only thus could they symbolize the sinless Son of God who was to come. We can compare this Chinese sacrifice with the instruction given by God to the Hebrews:

sheep, lamb

ox, bullock

> "Take a bull calf for a sin offering, and a
> ram for a burnt offering, both without
> blemish, and offer them before the Lord."²⁹

The combined information gained from both the Chinese and Hebrew sources amplifies the story related in the Hebrew record regarding the sacrifices offered years earlier by Adam's first two sons, Cain and Abel:

> Now Abel kept flocks, and Cain worked the soil. In
> the course of time Cain brought some of the fruits of
> the soil as an offering to the Lord. But Abel brought
> fat portions from some of the firstborn of his flock.
> The Lord looked with favor on Abel and his offering,
> but on Cain and his offering he did not look with
> favor. So Cain was very angry, and his face was
> downcast.³⁰

Cain was not bringing a proper animal sacrifice, and God would not accept it. Cain had a rebellious spirit. So, in a fit of jealousy, because Abel's offering of a lamb had been accepted, while his offerings of fruit were not, Cain killed his brother.

The Chinese record this act of murder in the character *cruel, violent, fierce* ⵣ ³¹ (兇). We see Cain pictured as the

cruel, violent, fierce

elder brother

elder brother 𦫖 [32](兄), who is taking hold of his younger brother, Abel 𠂉 (人). Note that there is a *mark* ✕ on Cain, In the Hebrew Scriptures it is recorded:

> And the Lord put a mark on Cain, lest
> any who came upon him should kill him.[33]

$$𦫖 \quad + \quad ✕ \quad + \quad 𠂉 \quad = \quad 𣎼$$

    elder brother   *mark*   *person (Abel)*   *violent, fierce*

Both *cruel* 𣎼 and *older brother* 𦫖 are pronounced *"hsiung."* The Lord drove Cain away. It is written that "Cain went out from the presence of the Lord."[34] He no longer worshiped at the *gate* 門 of Eden, where "God's presence" was manifested. Cain and his wife (his sister) became the ancestors of a rebellious race who hated God.

But there have been those throughout history who have honored the God of heaven. It was these who kept alive a knowledge of Him and His wonderful plan for the salvation of all people. The Hebrews were one of these people, worshiping El Shaddai (p. 14). It appears that the ancient Chinese were other believers in the Creator, whom they called ShangDi.

Although the significance of ShangDi, the original God of China, has been largely lost today , this sacred history of earth's beginnings was carefully recorded for all time in ancient Chinese pictographic writing. **Not only history is thus recorded, but also important prophetic information, as we will shortly learn.**

9

Confucius Pointed the Way

The new site for the worship of ShangDi was at the east gate of the Garden of Eden. This we learn from the Chinese characters and also from the Hebrew record, which reads:

> He drove out the man; and at the east of the garden of Eden he placed the cherubim [angels], and a flaming sword which turned every way, to guard the way to the tree of life.[1]

The original place of worship had been on the *mountain* Ⓜ (compare ⌄, ⌄, p. 33), the holy *hill* 𠂤 (陵 , p. 39) where Adam and Eve , in their newly-created sinless state, could *meet* 𒀭 (見 , p. 40) God face-to-face, eye-to-*eye* ▱ (目), on bended knee ⟩ as worshipers.

to meet

$$\text{⟩} \quad + \quad \text{▱} \quad = \quad \text{𒀭}$$

kneeling man   *eye*   *to meet*

After Adam and Eve had been expelled from Eden, a boundary had been set up at the gate to keep the first couple from the tree of life. The new location for worship, therefore, was at the

eye

garden *boundary, border* ² (囿). In , the worshiper is quite obvious as 㐱 . God is represented by 大 (大), a second "*noble* Man," the legs of which are melded with the legs of the *disobedient* 㐬 (㐬) noble man, Adam. The record of the Hebrews states: "The first man was of the earth, made of dust; the second Man is the Lord from heaven."³ This second *noble* 大 Man (also called the last Adam, the Savior) was to come and take the place of the first disobedient Adam.

boundary, border

$$ \text{大} \quad + \quad \text{㐬} \quad + \quad \text{㐱} \quad + \quad \square \quad = \quad \text{囿} $$

2nd noble Man   disobedient   worshiper   enclosure   border

(God the Son)   (Adam)

rejoice, give thanks to

Therefore, all people can *rejoice* and *give thanks to* 㚔 ⁴ (幸) the Savior, the last Adam.

$$ \text{大} \quad + \quad \text{㐬} \quad = \quad \text{㚔} $$

Noble Man (Savior)   disobedient   rejoice, give thanks to

grasp, take hold of

When the kneeling figure 㐱 is added, as 執⁵ (執), the new character means *grasp, take hold of.* All who desire to be saved from eternal death must *take hold of* 執 the Savior.

$$ \text{大} \quad + \quad \text{㐬} \quad = \text{㚔} + \quad \text{㐱} \quad = \quad \text{執} $$

Noble Man   disobedient   rejoice   kneeling man   take hold of

Finally, by placing this action at the *border* (囿) of Eden, we find depicted the original answer to Adam and Eve's plight. They came to Eden's *border* gate to worship the Savior.

Eden's gate was now the border or boundary past which

they were prevented from going by the presence of the cherubim angels. There are many additional Chinese characters meaning *border* or *boundary*. All have the same reference, the border of the Garden of Eden, more specifically, at the east gate.

Seed

We may conclude that the daily sacrificial service outside of Eden's east gate, was the "Border Sacrifice" initiated by ShangDi Himself. After Adam and Eve were driven from the garden, they could ask forgiveness for sin by a symbolic animal sacrifice at the border or gate of the Garden of Eden. The Border Sacrifice at Eden's closed gate looked forward to the sacrifice of the "*Seed* 孚 of the woman" (子 , p. 51) whose attributes are seen in the graph *bright as the shining sun* 㬎 [6] (杲). This portrays the promised Son's glory like the *sun's* 口 [7] (日).

$$\text{口} + \text{Y} + \text{|||} = \text{㬎}$$

| *Sun* | *God* | *God's presence* | *bright as shining sun* |

bright as the shining sun

We should not get the idea of a bloodthirsty god, demanding appeasement. Far from it, God the Father was to sacrifice His own Son for the benefit of humanity who were under the death penalty. Regarding God's feelings, the Hebrew writings make clear:

sun

> You do not delight in sacrifice, or I would bring it;
>   You do not take pleasure in burnt offerings.
> The sacrifices of God are a broken spirit;
>   a broken and contrite heart,
>   O God, You will not despise.[8]

In the Chinese Border Sacrifice, recall that the emperor

65

alone took a young, unblemished bull, slew it, and burned it upon an altar. The whole ceremony was accompanied by music and recitations to ShangDi, (some of which have been quoted in the first four chapters of this book). The emperor concluded the service by bowing low before the sacrificial altar in worship of ShangDi.

In performing this humble pose of worship, each emperor, over thousands of years, dynasty after dynasty, acknowledged his position as servant under Heaven. *Tian, Heaven* 夫 (天 p. 16), of course for the early Chinese, was a synonym for their God, ShangDi.

Heaven, God, Tian

Tian-ming, the Mandate of Heaven, stood for Heaven's rule over the people through the emperor. This divine-given rulership was granted with the provision that the emperor yielded to Heaven's laws. The graph 㝉 (令 p. 45) for *Mandate* pictures the obedient man 㔾 (卩), the emperor, under the command △ and protection of Heaven . (Adam had been this original obedient man 㔾 receiving the mandate. Compare pp. 44, 45). Confucius made this emperor's Mandate very clear throughout the Classics. For example, he wrote:

> Heaven, to protect the inferior people, made for
> them rulers, made for them teachers, that they may
> be able to assist ShangDi, to secure the peace of the
> four quarters [of the earth].[9]

Confucius' counsel to the good ruler was to know that God was with him, "to have no doubt nor anxiety, because ShangDi is with you."[10] Confucius pointed to King Wen, the father of the founder of the Zhou dynasty, as an exemplar for future rulers. King Wen was obedient to God, and in a manner remarkably similar to King David, who reigned in the Hebrew country of Judea about a century later, God spoke to King Wen:

> ShangDi said to King Wen,
> "I am pleased with your intelligent virtue,
> You do not proclaim it aloud nor portray it,
> You show no consciousness of effort,
> You act in accordance to ShangDi's laws."[11]

While the Mandate of Heaven, *Tian-ming,* referred to the divine origins of rulership, it also meant the "Will of Heaven," that is, the will of a personal God. This is what Confucius so reverently spoke of when he taught that one cannot be a "gentleman," a person of high moral character, unless one "knows this Will."[12] In regard to his own life, Confucius testified that not until the age of 50, did he receive this knowledge.

> The Master said,
> "At fifteen, I had my mind bent on learning.
> At thirty, I stood firm.
> At forty, I had no doubts.
> At fifty, *I knew the decrees of Heaven.*
> At sixty, my ear was an obedient organ for the reception of truth.
> At seventy, I could follow what my heart desired, without transgressing what was right."[13]

Throughout the five volumes of the Confucian Classics, but more prominent in the oldest two, the Book of Odes [詩經] and the Book of Historical Documents [書經], Confucius lifted up *Heaven* 天 (天) as the Supreme God. These texts reveal the original Confucian belief in God as the Creator:

67

> How vast is ShangDi,
> The ruler of men below.
> How arrayed in terrors is ShangDi:
> His ordinances are full of irregularities.
> Heaven gave birth to the multitudes of people…[14]

Confucius believed in Heaven as the source of all power, the authority of moral law, and a personal God who protected not only as a Ruler, but also as a Parent:

> Oh vast and distant Heaven,
> [You] who are called Father and Mother…[15]

This is THE GOD Confucius prayed to, and reportedly declared, "He who offends against Heaven has none to whom he can pray."[16] **For Confucius, there was no other God!**

Confucius' humility shines forth in these additional quotations:

> The Master said, "The sage and the man of perfect virtue;—how dare I rank myself with them? It may be simply said of me, that I strive to become such without satiety, and teach others without weariness."[17]

> The Master said, "When I walk along with two others, they may serve me as my teachers. I will select their good qualities and follow them, their bad qualities and avoid them."[18]

> The Master said, "Heaven *[Tian, God]* produced the virtue that is in me."[19]

From compiling the classical texts, Confucius had the knowledge of the ancient documents and odes of the Shang and possibly earlier texts. With this knowledge he exclaimed:

"He who understands the ceremonies of the
sacrifices to Heaven and Earth ... would find the
government of a kingdom as easy as to look into his
palm!"[20]

In Confucius' day, about 500 B.C., at least 1700 years had
already passed since the dynastic rule of China was established.
These early rulers, it appears, understood the religious prin-
ciples that had been handed down by word of mouth from the
time of creation. The ancient sage who had invented the written language also had true concepts of the history of the world.
He recorded this knowledge for all time in his pictographic
characters. The Xia and Shang dynasties had passed, and now,
during Confucius' lifetime, the famed Zhou dynasty was ruling
China. Because of the long passage of time, therefore, a true
knowledge of ShangDi had dimmed. The Border Sacrifice,
part of the worship of ShangDi, had survived to become a magnificent imperial ritual,but had lost its original purpose.

As we have briefly reviewed the history of Adam and Eve,
we found that their unfortunate act of disobedience and disloyalty meant the death sentence. But God had proposed to
ransom them by sending a Savior to be born as the *Seed* 子
(子, p. 51)of the woman. In the plan, this Savior would crush
the head of the serpent (蛇, p. 51), that old enemy of God,
the devil. However, the Savior Himself would be "bitten in the
heel." What did this mean?

When Adam and Eve left their beautiful garden home in
Eden, ShangDi had lovingly provided garments of skins for
them. These *robes* 衣 (衣, pp. 57-59) made necessary the

death of innocent sacrificial animals, likely *sheep* 个 (羊 p. 58), to cover their nakedness. The *Lamb* was a symbol of the coming Savior. The sacrifice of this animal was to represent the Savior's death and payment for their sentence, "You will surely die." The sinless Savior would substitute His life for sinful humanity.

"You will not die" had been the devil's promise to Eve. Who would be right, ShangDi or the devil? Death has come upon all people, from Adam's son, Abel, the first to die, to our very day.

God had told Adam he would return to dust. Death is the opposite of creation, as we may learn in a quote from the Hebrew text:

> When You take away their breath,
> they die and return to the dust.
> When You send Your Spirit,
> they are created.[21]

Compare also:

> When his breath departs, he returns to his earth;
> on that very day his plans perish.[22]

But there is hope that the dead will live again. This is ShangDi's wonderful promise for salvation. God's own Son would one day be born on earth as the *Seed* 予 of the woman, live a sinless life among people, and give His life for all people who allow themselves to be covered by the *righteousness* 𦍋 (義 , p. 58) of this heavenly sacrifice. There will be a day when all the righteous dead will live again according to this Hebrew record:

70

And many of those who sleep in the dust of the earth shall awake, some to everlasting life, and some to shame and everlasting contempt. And those who are wise shall shine like the brightness of the firmament; and those who turn many to righteousness, like the stars for ever and ever.[23]

In Confucius' day, that supreme sacrifice had not yet been made. The promised Seed of the woman, the Savior of all humanity, had not yet come. But about 200 years before the time of Confucius, a Hebrew prophet had looked far down into the future, writing in past tense as though the event had already happened. Listen to this highly descriptive and detailed picture that he foretold of the Savior to come:

Who would have believed what we now report?
  Who could have seen the Lord's hand in this?
It was the will of the Lord that His servant
  grow like a plant taking root in dry ground....
We despised Him and rejected Him;
  He endured suffering and pain.
No one would even look at Him—
  we ignored Him as if He were nothing.
But He endured the suffering that should have been ours,
  the pain that we should have borne... .
Because of our sins He was wounded,
  beaten because of the evil we did.
We are healed by the punishment He suffered,
  made whole by the blows He received.
All of us were like sheep that were lost,
  each of us going his own way.
But the Lord made the punishment fall on Him,
  the punishment all of us deserved.
He was treated harshly, but endured it humbly;
  He never said a word... .
He was arrested and sentenced and led off to die,
  and no one cared about His fate.
He was put to death for the sins of our people.

> He was placed in a grave with evil men,
>> he was buried with the rich,
>
> even though He had never committed a crime
>> or ever told a lie.
>
> The Lord says,
> "It was My will that He should suffer;
>> His death was a **sacrifice** to bring forgiveness....
>> and through Him my purpose will succeed.
>
> After a life of suffering, He will again have joy;
>> He will know that He did not suffer in vain.
>
> My devoted servant, with whom I am pleased,
>> will bear the punishment of many
>> and for His sake I will forgive them.
>
> And so I will give Him a place of honor,
>> a place among great and powerful men.
>
> He willingly gave His life
>> and shared the fate of evil men.
>
> He took the place of many sinners
>> and prayed that they might be forgiven."[24]

This promise had not yet been fulfilled in Confucius' day; it was still future for ShangDi's purposes to be realized.

The Han dynasty followed the famed Zhou dynasty of Confucius' era. During the reign of Emperor Ai 哀帝 (6 B.C.-1 A.D., and perhaps his name meaning "to pity, to sympathize with" was prophetic), a son was born to a humble peasant couple. Joseph and Mary lived in a far-distant land. On a map, locate, east of the Mediterranean Sea, the country of Israel. This was the ancient land of the Hebrews, whose Scriptures we have been comparing with the Chinese character-writing. In a small Judean town of Bethlehem, an event of great importance to the whole world took place. But many strange things happened simultaneously with the birth of this special baby.

10

The Seed
of the Woman

The first in a series of strange events was the appearance of a heavenly angel to a lovely young woman, Mary, with an important message. Mary was looking forward to her approaching marriage with Joseph. Both were descendants of King David, in the royal Judean line (see p. 67). But it had been centuries since a Judean king had ruled over Israel. Indeed, at that time (about 2,000 years ago), their nation was under the tyrannical rule of Rome. Joseph was, instead of a prince, a humble carpenter in the town of Nazareth.

The visit of an angel was a rare event of great honor, and the heavenly messenger put aside Mary's fears by saying:

> "Don't be afraid, Mary; God has been gracious to you. You will become pregnant and give birth to a son, and you will name Him *Jesus. He will be great and will be called the Son of the Most High God.* The Lord God will make Him a king, as His ancestor David was … His kingdom will never end!"[1]

Perplexed, Mary spoke to the angel, "I am a virgin. How, then, can this be?"[2]

> The angel answered, "The Holy Spirit [the third member of the Godhead] will come on you, and God's power will rest upon you. For this reason the holy child will be called the Son of God" [the second member of the Godhead].[3] (See 丁 , pp. 17, 18; 㶟 33; 早 51, 65; 个 58-61).

Mary responded, "I am the Lord's servant, ... may it happen to me as you have said."[4]

An angel also visited Joseph, reassuring him:

> "Joseph, descendant of David, do not be afraid to take Mary to be your wife. For it is by the Holy Spirit that she has conceived. She will have a son, and you will name Him Jesus—because *He will save His people from their sins.*"[5]

So Joseph took Mary as his wife, but he had not consummated the marriage. A few months later, a great census was being taken throughout the Roman Empire. All were required to register in the hometown of their family's ancestral leader. Thus Joseph and Mary journeyed to Bethlehem, the ancient town of their ancestor, King David.

Bethlehem, they found upon their arrival, was so crowded with travelers that there were no empty inn rooms. The best they could do was to find a sleeping place on the sweet-smelling hay in a barn. It was under these humble conditions that Jesus, the long-awaited "*Seed* 早 of the woman," was born to this poor peasant couple.

The human family had known predictions of a promised Savior since Adam and Eve were expelled from the Garden of Eden. Yet how many expected Him at this time? In the Hebrew sacred writings, there were many prophecies foretelling that Jesus, the Son of God, would come to earth. Daniel, a prince and prophet living as a captive in Babylon during Confucius' own lifetime, had written of the time when the Savior would appear. But only a few had bothered to study the Hebrew Scriptures sufficiently to learn when this might be. These faithful ones knew His coming must be soon. Among the expectant believers were simple shepherds who often talked of the Savior and what His coming would be like. As these herdsmen were watching their flocks in the countryside one night, an angel appeared to them also, joyously announcing:

> "Don't be afraid! I am here with good news for you, which will bring great joy to all the people. This very day in David's town your Savior was born—Christ the Lord! And this is what will prove it to you: you will find a baby wrapped in cloths and lying in a manger."[6]

Then appeared to the amazed shepherds a great host of angels singing and rejoicing. The angels directed the shepherds to where Mary, Joseph, and the Baby were—not to a palace, but to an animal shed.

The Child had other visitors as well. Wise men arrived from the east. They asked of the ruler, Herod, "Where is He who has been born King of the Jews? For we have seen His star in the East and have come to worship Him."[7] They had learned that a special star would arise in the heavens to announce the birth of a Savior. When it had appeared, they followed the moving star a great distance and finally reached Jerusalem. As King Herod heard these things, he was greatly upset and called together the chief priests and teachers to ask where this Savior was to be born. They read for him the prophecy that had been written hundreds of years before:

> "*Bethlehem* Ephrathah, you are one of the smallest towns in Judah, but out of you I will bring a ruler for Israel, whose family line goes back to ancient times."...

> When He comes, He will rule His people with the strength that comes from the Lord and with the majesty of the Lord God Himself. His people will live in safety because *people all over the earth will acknowledge His greatness*, and He will bring peace.[8]

Herod was so disturbed by this word that he determined to destroy the Child who would possibly depose him from his throne. Without revealing his evil intentions, Herod lied to the wise men, "Go and make a careful search for the child; and when you find Him, let me know, so that I too may go and worship Him."[9]

The wise men continued to follow the star to the very house where Mary and Joseph were now living. The visitors from the east entered the house and knelt before the Child. They gave gifts of gold, frankincense, and myrrh, which they had brought with them. The men, being warned in a dream not to return to Herod, then left for their own country by another route.

Again an angel appeared to Joseph with the warning to take his family immediately to Egypt. This he did—and none too soon, for Herod sent his soldiers with the order to kill all the boys of two years and younger in the region of Bethlehem. The gifts of the wise men possibly helped support the family while in Egypt, where they stayed until the death of the wicked king Herod. Then they returned to Nazareth.

When Jesus was 12 years old, Joseph and Mary took Him with them to the yearly Passover Festival in Jerusalem. On their way home, they suddenly realized the Boy was not with their company of travelers. They returned to Jerusalem and spent the next three days frantically searching for Him. At last they decided to look in the temple, and there they heard His voice. He was

> sitting with the Jewish teachers, listening to them and asking questions. All who heard Him were amazed at His intelligent answers.... His mother said to Him, "Son, why have You done this to us? Your father and I have been terribly worried trying to find You."
>
> He answered them, "Why did you have to look for Me? Didn't you know that I had to be in My Father's house?" But they did not understand His answer."[10]

Jesus identified Himself with God, calling Him "Father," and the temple He named as "God's house." Was Jesus inquiring of the priests about the significance of the sheep sacrifices that He had witnessed in the temple? We do not know. He returned then to Nazareth with His parents.

Nothing more is known of the childhood and youth of Jesus, who grew to manhood working in Joseph's carpenter shop in Nazareth. One short statement summarized this period of His life: "The child grew and became strong; He was full of wisdom, and God's blessings were upon Him."[11] We do know that His life from the beginning was empowered by the Holy Spirit within Him, so that He lived a life totally without sin. No other person on earth has ever been able to do this.

At the age of 30, Jesus left the carpenter's bench and went to Jerusalem. Shortly thereafter, He was baptized in the Jordan River by His relative John, who had become a famous preacher. Following the public baptism of Jesus, John announced, "There is the Lamb of God, who takes away the sin of the world!"[12] Why did John identify Jesus with this animal used as a sacrifice in Jerusalem's temple services? We will soon understand.

Jesus then began His work that He had come into the world to do. Immediately the devil came to Him with a series of grueling temptations, far worse than the simple temptation that had led Adam and Eve to disobey God. Satan was eager to overcome the Son of God in His vulnerable human form. But unlike Adam and Eve, Jesus overcame each test by relying upon the power that God gave Him. He did not separate Himself from the Father's ever-present help as Adam and Eve had. As a Man, He also understood, from His knowledge of the Hebrew Scriptures, the truth about the war between God and Lucifer (Satan, the devil).

Jesus chose 12 ordinary men of various ages and

occupations to be His disciples. Several were fishermen; one was a tax collector. Jesus' righteous character, His forthright teachings, and His mastery of every situation attracted them. He had great compassion, and as He passed from town to town, His fame as a great healer preceded Him. Sick people with every kind of hopeless disease were brought to Jesus. By divine miracles, He immediately brought all back to complete health and soundness of body and mind. Often after He had healed them, He said, "Your sins are forgiven; go and sin no more."

He taught about God's coming kingdom by telling stories with deep meaning, drawing illustrations from current happenings or from nature. His work for others was tireless. Yet He had enemies—the religious leaders. "How can this unlearned carpenter forgive sins? By what authority does He teach the people and especially forgive sins? Only God has the power and right to remove sin. How dare this mere man assume the authority that only God has!" So thought these men who tried over and over to trap Him in a misstatement, an untruth, an inconsistency of life or teaching.

Always Jesus showed the utmost wisdom and insight in dealing with them. However, He did not hesitate to point out their errors in a direct manner, which only further angered them.

On three occasions Jesus raised people from death to life again. One of those resurrected, a dear friend, had been dead and entombed for four days. Again the religious leaders attempted to discredit these acts as mere magic, done under the influence of the devil.

79

In spite of the controversy with these leaders, Jesus was popular and greatly loved by the common people. Some of them were convinced that He must be the long-awaited Savior, the Seed of the woman, sent from God. Jesus' public ministry lasted only three-and-a-half years, ending when one of His own disciples betrayed Him.

The day of the great, national yearly celebration, the Passover Feast, drew close. When 12 years old, Jesus had observed this event in Jerusalem with His parents. In commemoration of the Hebrews' deliverance from Egyptian slavery centuries before, the Passover was still annually kept. This had been not only a historical escape from bondage, but it had also symbolized the eventual release of God's people from the captivity of Satan and sin.

Under the guidance of God and the leadership of Moses, each Hebrew family that first Passover evening in Egypt had killed a lamb. They had been directed to wipe its blood over the doorways of their houses. This was a sign for God's destroying angel to *pass over* their houses, when the firstborn of all the Egyptians were to be slain. The lamb's blood was a sign that the Hebrew firstborn were to be saved from death in that crisis hour. Moreover, the Hebrews ate the flesh of the roasted lamb, but no bones in its body were to be broken. This entire epic bore deep symbolic meaning.

Since that time, the ceremony had been repeated each year with the sacrifice and eating of the Passover lamb. In Jesus' day, the Hebrews still conducted the ritual (in addition to the daily morning and evening lamb sacrifices in Jerusalem's temple). Lambs and oxen had been sacrificed from the time of Adam at Eden's border gate, pointing forward to this very time. Even in China, a yearly Border Sacrifice was conducted, though its significance was no longer understood.

On the evening before the Passover, Thursday night, Jesus called His 12 disciples together in the upper room of a house. While they all sat at a table, He "took a piece of bread, gave thanks to God, broke it, and said, 'This is My body, which is [broken] for you.'"[13] Then each of the men ate portions of the bread. Eating of the Passover lamb had also symbolized the body of Jesus, which was soon to be "broken."

blood

Next, Jesus passed around sweet wine for each to drink, saying, "This is My blood, ... [which is] poured out for many for the forgiveness of sins. I tell you, I will never again drink this wine until the day I drink the new wine with you in My Father's Kingdom."[14] But the disciples failed at first to understand the deep significance of the service.

The character for *blood*  (血 , p. 60) shows ◇ , the holy "flame" being poured into a *vessel* , [15] (皿) composed of two conjoined *persons* ⌒ + ⌒ . Jesus' blood was to be "poured out for many"—not only for Adam and Eve, but for all mankind.

vessel

◇ + (vessel) = (blood)

holy, flame   vessel   blood

In the figure , we can also see the origin of (主 , p. 60), *Lord, Master*, the God ⅄ who will give His life *blood*.

Lord, Master

$$\text{Ψ} \quad + \quad \text{(o)} \quad = \quad \text{Ψ̈}$$

God   blood   Lord, Master

After leaving the room that evening, Jesus and His friends, except for one disciple, Judas, who had excused himself early, went to a garden to pray. However, sleep overcame all His followers, and Jesus alone prayed to the Father in heaven for strength to go through the ordeal He faced on behalf of all people.

While Jesus was still there in the garden, a noisy crowd approached and, from their midst, the missing disciple Judas stepped forth and kissed Jesus, in order to betray Him. At this signal, Jesus was arrested and taken prisoner. Suddenly He was alone in the hands of an angry mob, for all His disciples had fled.

Now read once more the amazing details of the prophecy recorded over 500 years before regarding the events that were to occur this night (pp. 71-72). **The time had come!**

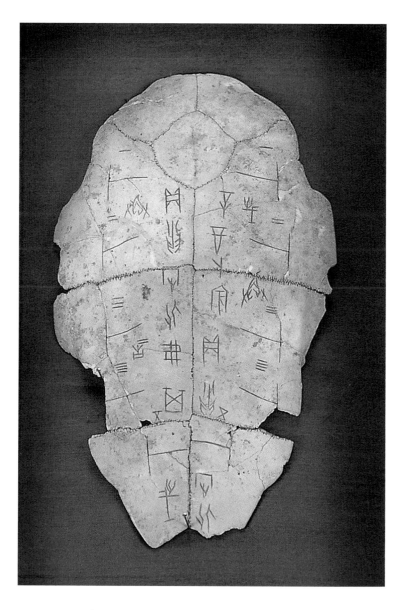

Oracle Bone writing on a tortoise plastron
(Courtesy of Mr. Wen-Lu Wang, Academia Sinica, Taipei)

② ③ ①

The Temple and Altar of Heaven Complex in Beijing

①

Hall of Prayer for Good Harvests

②

Imperial Vault (Temple of Heaven)

③

Tourists atop Altar of Heaven

"Heavenly Sovereign ShangDi." Inscription in the Imperial Vault
(Temple of Heaven), and in the Hall of Prayer for Good Harvests.

11

Original Purpose of the Altar of Heaven

It was before dawn on Friday morning. Jesus, with hands bound, was led through the dark and empty streets of Jerusalem toward the house of the high priest. A number of teachers of the law and other religious leaders had gathered in his home at this unusual hour. As an unofficial, assembled council, they attempted to find some crime of which to accuse Jesus, so that they could demand His death.

Many false witnesses came forward with lying statements. These seemed insufficient, until finally two men stepped up and reported, "This man said, 'I am able to tear down God's Temple and three days later build it back up.' "[1] Immediately the high priest demanded that Jesus reply to this accusation. When He remained silent,

> the high priest said to Him, "I charge You under oath by the living God: Tell us if You are the Christ, the Son of God."

> "Yes, it is as you say," Jesus replied, "But I say to all

of you: In the future you will see the Son of Man
sitting at the right hand of the Mighty One and
coming on the clouds of heaven."[2]

In horror, the high priest tore his priestly garments and
cried, "Blasphemy! This man claims to be God! You have just
heard Him. What do you think?"

They all answered, "He is guilty and must die!" So they spat
in His face and slapped and beat Him. They put Him in chains
and led Him off to the Roman governor, for the Jews could not,
by themselves, effect His execution, since they were under
Roman rule.

Next, Pontius Pilate, the Roman governor questioned Him,

"Are you the king of the Jews?" And He answered
him and said, "It is as you say."

Then Pilate said to the chief priests and the crowd,
"I find no fault in this Man."[3]

The governor declined to make a decision, sending Him
off instead to Herod the local ruler over the region. Having
heard much about Jesus, Herod hoped to see Him perform
some miracles. He asked Him many questions, but Jesus remained silent. Because Jesus did not respond to their purpose-
less inquiries, Herod and his soldiers treated Him with contempt. In mockery, they put a purple robe and a crown of
twisted thorn twigs on Him, then sent Him back to Pilate.

Now Pilate could no longer postpone his decision. He said
to the Jewish religious leaders,

"I have not found Him guilty of any of the crimes
you accuse Him of. Nor did Herod find Him guilty,

for he sent him back to us. There is nothing this man has done to deserve death. So I will have Him whipped and let Him go."[4]

But the gathering crowd cried out, "Kill Him!"

Pilate wanted to set Jesus free, and since it was the custom at Passover time to free whatever prisoner the crowd demanded be released, he asked them, "Shall I set free the criminal Barabbas or Jesus?"

The crowd, influenced by the religious leaders, demanded Barabbas be freed and Jesus be put to death. When Pilate realized a riot might break out if he did not comply with the wishes of the people, he took some water and washed his hands before them saying, "I am not responsible for the death of this man! This is your doing!"[5]

So, through a great failure of justice, this noble Man, the Son of God, was lashed by Roman whips until His back was torn and bleeding. Blows to the head drove the thorny crown into His brow, until the blood streamed down His face. They spit on Him and then made Him carry His own heavy wooden cross, for crucifixion was the method of execution used by the cruel Romans. Calvary, the place of crucifixion, was on a small hill. Weak from the torture and abuse that had been heaped upon Him, Jesus could no longer carry the cross. A stranger from a foreign country was made to carry the cross for Him.

Calvary was located outside Jerusalem's gate. How important this fact is! The Bible relates:

> So Jesus also suffered *outside the gate* in order to sanctify the people through His own blood.[6]

Even as Adam's sacrifice of unblemished lambs had been made outside Eden's gate, so also Jesus, the Lamb of God, was offered outside of Jerusalem, the holy Hebrew city. This too was a fulfillment of the ancient Chinese Border Sacrifice, the "border" being Eden's gate, typifying Jerusalem's gate where the great sacrifice for all humanity was to be made.

Roman soldiers laid out Jesus on the cross, nailing His hands, as well as his feet, to the rough wooden cross beneath. They then unmercifully dropped the cross into a prepared hole in the ground, which caused the weight of His body to tear the flesh of His hands and feet into gaping wounds. He took all the abuse without an outcry. He even murmured, "Forgive them, Father! They don't know what they are doing."[7] The crosses of two thieves, scheduled for execution at the same time, stood on either side of the central cross where Jesus hung.

Picture the scene. Three crosses are silhouetted on a hill against a darkening sky. On the highest, central cross hangs the Son of God. As we see the Savior *hanging with outstretched, upraised arms*, held fast by the cruel nails through His hands, we remember a familiar figure Ⓨ, representing God. Remember the symbols of ShangDi with arms upraised in blessing: 田 (p. 27); 㐁 (p. 39)? This God Ⓨ is Jesus Christ, also symbolized by Ⓨ (主, p. 81); Ⓨ (羊, p. 58); Ⓨ (牛 , p. 61).

One name of Jesus was Immanuel, "God with Us."[8] The

name Jesus itself means, "Savior"[9] What greater blessing is there than the sacrifice Jesus was making at that hour for all humanity?

It was 9 A.M., the time of the morning sacrifice of the lamb in the temple, when Jesus was hung upon the cross. He suffered anguish from terrible physical pain, but far worse, **He bore the crushing sins of all humanity.** Our sins that He bore separated Him from God the Father. He cried out, "My God, My God, why have You forsaken Me?"[10]

"For He [the Father-God] made Him [Jesus] who knew no sin to be sin for us, that we might become the righteousness of God in Him."[11]

As Jesus endured the pain and mockery of the cross, He was dying the sinners' death—that death which is a solitary one, without God. He died for lost humanity of all generations, from Adam and Eve's time—and yes, even into the future, to the end of time.

It was 3 P.M., the hour for slaying the sacrificial animals in the evening, when Jesus spoke His last words, "It is finished,"[12] and breathed His last.

The sacrifice of the ages was complete. Every unblemished lamb or bull offered in the past had pointed forward to this very hour. It was the very moment in time and the act that had so intrigued the sage Confucius. The sacrificial death of Jesus had been represented by thousands of burning bulls offered by successive emperors of China at the annual Border Sacrifice. Even in our 20th century, this ancient rite was still being conducted at Beijing's Altar of Heaven.

All nature convulsed as its Creator died. There was a mighty earthquake. Strange things happened

> Then the curtain hanging in the Temple was torn in two from top to bottom. The earth shook, the rocks split apart, the graves broke open, and many of God's people who had died were raised to life. They left the graves, and after Jesus rose from death, they went into the Holy City, where many people saw them.[13]

The tearing of the magnificent curtain in the temple indicated a completion of the sacrificial service there conducted. The Lamb of God, to whom all the temple services pointed, had been slain. Henceforth, all sacrifices would be meaningless.

But in China, what had transpired outside the gates of Jerusalem, nearly 2,000 years ago, was completely unknown. China's emperors continued slaying unblemished bulls at the great Border Sacrifice year after year until 1911 when the last emperor was deposed.

The reigning ruler of China at the time of Jesus' death was Emperor Kuang Wu 光武帝 .[14] Perhaps his name, "The Hero of Light," was also prophetic. Many thousands of miles away from China, unbeknown to the Chinese, the world's greatest hero of all time had given His life for the world.

Jesus never called Himself a hero, but He had said, "I am the light of the world.... Whoever follows Me will have the light of life and will never walk in darkness."[15] One of His disciples later said of Him, "That was the true Light which gives light to every man who comes into the world."[16]

Sadly, that same disciple also wrote that Jesus had been rejected by the very ones He came to save:

> He was in the world, and the world was made through Him, and the world did not know Him. He came to His own, and His own did not receive Him.[17]

A bold Roman soldier, not being certain whether Jesus had indeed died, thrust a spear into His side as He hung on the cross, and out flowed blood and water. A *spring, fountain* 羆 (泉 , pp. 32-33) of blood and water gushed from the gashed side of Jesus. This character 羆 now becomes even more meaningful as we find the *water* ⺡ (水 , p. 33), representing the "water of life," pouring from God 丁 (示).

Examine also the characters 牢 , 牢 [18] (牢) meaning *sacrificial animals.* How significant that the blood of the sacrificial animals, the *sheep* 羊 and the *bulls* 牛 **would flow as a spring, fountain!**

sacrificial animals

> In that day a *fountain* shall be opened. . . for sin and for uncleanness.[19]

For thousands of years, *sheep* 羊 (羊) and *bull* 牛 (牛) offerings had been made, looking forward to the sacrificial death of the sinless Son of God, Jesus, when His *blood* 血 (血 , p. 81) would flow for all of sinful, repentant mankind.

His death, Jesus had promised, would mean *eternal*

丮 [20](永) life for everyone who would believe that He truly was the Son of God. Recall the bifurcation of the four rivers 彳亍 (行, p.32) on the Holy Mount. How appropriate that the inventor of Chinese writing, more than 2,000 years before, had written *eternal* 丮 to resemble the flowing *water* 氵 (水)of the River of Life! The graph 彳 (行) which means *to walk* shows the one way that leads to this *water* 氵 of life. When you look closely at 丮 , you will see God (Jesus) as a *man* 亻 in its center. He is the true source of eternal life.

eternal

$$ 彳 \quad + \quad 亻 \quad + \quad 氵 \quad = \quad 丮 $$

to walk	*Person*	*water*	*eternal*

Jesus, by His death, has invited all to inherit everlasting life.

> And the Spirit. . .say[s], "Come!" And let him who hears say, "Come!" And let him who thirsts come. And whoever desires, let him take the water of life freely.[21]

Although only the Son of God suffered on the cross, this sacrifice was a precious gift to humanity from the whole Triune Godhead.

> For God so loved the world that He gave His only Son, that whoever believes in Him should not perish but have eternal life.[22]

For Jesus' disciples, the darkest hour had come. They were not remembering Jesus' words pronounced at the last supper with Him in the upper room. They had eaten bread and drunk sweet wine, of which Jesus said, "This is My body" and "this is My blood, which seals God's covenant, My blood poured out for many for the forgiveness of sins."[23] They, instead, had built their hopes upon His becoming a king who would throw off the Roman rule. Even His disciples did not then understand His true universal mission on behalf of all humanity around the earth, and not for Israel alone.

Two wealthy and heretofore secret friends and believers of Jesus now came forward to claim His body. Not one bone of His body had been broken. If He had not died before sunset, the soldiers would have broken His legs to hasten His death. Recall that no bones of the Passover lamb were to be broken. Jesus was that Lamb.

Those eminent men now wrapped His body in strips of cloth and placed Him in a new tomb, cut out of a rock, which had actually been purchased for one of them. A great stone was rolled before the opening. Roman guards posted at the request of the high priest watched the tomb to prevent His disciples from stealing away the body. The religious leaders remembered Jesus saying on a number of occasions that He would be resurrected on the third day: "Destroy this temple [My body], and I will raise it again in three days."[24]

The weekly seventh day of rest, commemorating God's original six days of work in creating the earth and all plant and animal life, was drawing on as the sun set in the western sky. This Sabbath, the world's Creator *rested* Ʋ (止) in the tomb. He had accomplished for humanity His appointed mission of making possible the re-creation of each person's character through His own gift of *righteousness* 𦍌 (義, p. 58), open to all people, all the descendants of Adam.

> For just as all people die because of their union
> with Adam, in the same way all will be raised to life
> because of their union with Christ [Jesus].[25]

Very early on the third day after His death, an angel descended from heaven and rolled back the great stone from the mouth of the tomb. Guarding Roman soldiers dropped as dead men at the dazzling brightness of the angel. Jesus stepped from the tomb—the resurrected Savior. The fallen "Temple of God" had indeed been restored, according to His promise.

The risen Son of God appeared to His disciples and many others for 40 days after His resurrection. Then one day

> When He had led them out to the vicinity of Bethany,
> He *lifted up His hands and blessed them.*[26]

Our final picture of Jesus, the Son of God, is of Him on the Mount of Olives, with upraised arms in blessing. Recall the character *voice* 㕯 (聲 , p. 39). It was the same posture ShangDi, from the very beginning, had taken on the Holy Mount 厂 . Now Jesus' disciples were to hear for the last time the voice of Jesus.

> "You shall receive power when the Holy Spirit has
> come upon you; and you shall be witnesses to Me in
> Jerusalem, and in all Judea and Samaria, *and to the
> end of the earth.* "[27]

As His followers watched, Jesus began to rise from the earth. An Angel announced to the disciples: "This Jesus, who was taken from you into heaven, will come back in the same way that you saw Him go to heaven."[28]

Today, 2,000 years later, we must seriously ponder: Does all this have meaning for me?

12

ShangDi's Last Promise

In the second chapter of this little book, the question was asked, "Where did we come from?" But there are other equally puzzling questions frequently contemplated by most individuals: "Why am I here?" "Is there more to life than this?" "Will I live again after this life?" In other words, "Where am I going?"

Jesus, the Son of God, said to His disciples while He was here on earth:

> "Do not be worried and upset.... Believe in God and believe also in Me. There are many rooms in My Father's house, and I am going to prepare a place for you. I would not tell you this if it were not so. And after I go and prepare a place for you, I will come back and take you to Myself, so that you will be where I am....
>
> "No one goes to the Father except by Me."[1]

The Hebrew Scriptures, which we have been quoting, eventually became the first portion of the Christian's Holy Bible.

After the death, resurrection and return of Jesus Christ to heaven, His disciples wrote of Christ's life and teachings which became the second part of the Bible. Perhaps by now you are convinced, as are we, that the original God of China, ShangDi, is identical with the Hebrew and Christian God of the Bible.

In the Bible, we can read more about the place in heaven where Jesus returned to and is still living today. The Bible describes a beautiful heavenly city called the New Jerusalem. It has a great high wall with 12 pearly gates. The New Jerusalem is perfectly square and its height is equal to its length and breadth. The city itself is of pure gold, clear as glass, and its wall is made of jasper. Twelve kinds of shining jewels are set in the 12 foundations of the wall, giving it a rainbow effect.[2] In this city, Jesus is called "the Lamb," because of His sacrifice for earth's people. Those whose names are written in the "Lamb's Book of Life"—those who accept Jesus as their Savior from sin—can one day enter the city.

In the middle of the city is ShangDi/God's throne. From the throne flows the river of life, and on either side of the river is the tree of life.[3] God's throne is located on the majestic Mount Zion.

> Then I looked, and behold, a Lamb [Jesus] standing on Mount Zion, and with Him one hundred and forty-four thousand, ... [and] they sang as it were a new song before the throne.[4]
>
> The Lord reigns; ... He dwells between the cherubim; ... The Lord is great in Zion, and He is high above all the peoples.[5]

94

But wait a minute! Was there not a tree of life in the Garden of Eden, Adam and Eve's first home on earth? Yes. In addition, based on the premise that the Chinese characters convey historical fact, we believe that there was also a physical holy mountain in Eden.

The graph for *garden* ⊞ accurately pictures the four rivers arising from the center of the square garden. In other words, the garden of Eden was an earthly miniature replica of the city of ShangDi/God in heaven. The ancient symbol for *garden* 畄 (甫 , p. 27) depicts God Ψ , with arms upraised, in the very center of the garden. The source of the rivers was the *fountain, spring* 鼏 (泉 , pp. 32,31) of life, a unique symbol for the source of all life in ShangDi/God ⊤ Himself.

In the early chapters, ShangDi was identified as the Creator of heaven, earth, and all living things on the earth. Both the venerable Chinese Border Sacrifice recitations (pp. 4, 5, ,8, 9, 19) and the ancient pictographic Chinese characters verified His creatorship. ShangDi commanded all things into existence (p. 19). Jesus is also identified as the Creator in the Holy Bible, where He is called the "Word," because He too *spoke* everything into existence:

> Before the world was created, the Word already
> existed; He was with God, and He was the same as
> God. From the very beginning the Word was with
> God. *Through Him God made all things; not one
> thing in all creation was made without Him.* The
> Word was the source of life, and this life brought
> light to mankind. ...

> The Word was in the world, and though *God made the world through Him,* yet the world did not recognize Him. He came to His own country, but His own people did not receive Him. Some, however, did receive Him and believed in Him; so He gave them the right to become God's children.

> The Word became a human being and, full of grace and truth, lived among us. We saw his glory, the glory which he received as the Father's only Son.[6]

Note that, through the "Word" (Jesus), God made all things. Jesus, the Son, was God the Father's agent in His creative work. The Spirit was also an agent in creation. The three Persons of the Godhead worked as one in creating our world.

Jesus Himself had declared, "The Father and I are one."[7] This is indeed a strange statement, and even His disciples did not immediately understand it. One disciple, Philip, asked, "Lord, show us the Father and that will be enough for us." To this Jesus replied:

rain, "Holy Spirit"

> "Anyone who has seen Me has seen the Father.... Don't you believe that I am in the Father, and that the Father is in Me? The words I say to you are not just My own. Rather, it is the Father, living in Me, who is doing His work."[7]

The Spirit, as just mentioned, was also an agent in creation, and this activity, too, is explicitly seen in the oracle bone characters: *rain* 〔⺲〕 (雨 , see explanation on p. 18 where "rain" is equated with the Spirit).

Therefore, we can say that although the Godhead represents three separate Persons, yet their purposes are one and their work is one. We believe that the Chinese Trinity is exactly the same as the Hebrew/Christian Godhead, consisting of the all-powerful Creator, Savior, and Sustainer of the earth: the Ruler of the entire universe.

Is it any accident that when Jesus, the Son, gave His life as the *Lamb* 𐓗 of God in sacrifice for humanity's sins, that He was nailed to a cross, a *tree* 𝕏 ? This ugly *tree* 𝕏 of suffering has become the "tree of life" and immortality for all obedient believers. In God's beautiful new city, there is no tree of the knowledge of good and evil. Recall that this tree formerly stood next to the tree of life in the center of the earthly garden. There will be no temptation in the new Garden of Eden, the holy city, for Satan (the devil, the old serpent) will have been forever eliminated.

Jesus has promised to return to our earth again. Rebellious humanity has departed far from righteousness and followed the devil's example instead. The result has been war, bloodshed, crime, unfaithfulness, and misery. The devil has had his opportunity to demonstrate his kind of dominion and government on the earth. And now, once more, ShangDi/God will end the reign of sin on earth, as He did by the war in heaven against Satan (see p. 43).

How can one be saved from the destruction and death that will sweep over the entire earth? The only safe hiding *place* 𐓷 9 (區) will be in God's care. 匚 10 (匚) means *to*

97

conceal, hide. The three *person(s)* ⊔ are identified as the Trinity, the Godhead. This safe *place* 𝘭𝘢 of *hiding* ⊏ is only with God. The end of all things is fast approaching.

a place

While Jesus was on earth, His disciples came to Him with the question, "What will be the sign of Your coming, and of the end of the age?"[11] So He gave them a list of events to look for:

conceal, hide

- False Christs and false prophets will deceive many.
- Wars and rumors of wars; nation rising against nations
- Famines, pestilences, and earthquakes in various places
- Persecution of righteous people
- Lawlessness will increase.
- Life will go on as usual, most people unaware of approaching doom because of unbelief in God.
- The good news of Salvation through Jesus Christ will be brought to every nation, and then the end will come.[12]

No one need be ignorant of what is coming upon the earth. The Bible is full of warnings. But we are told that few will believe Jesus is really coming again—soon.

> You must understand that in the last days some people … will make fun of you and will ask, "He promised to come, didn't He? Where is He? Our fathers have already died, but everything is still the same as it was since the creation of the world!" …
> But the heavens and the earth that now exist are being preserved by the same command of God, in order to be destroyed by fire. They are being kept for the day when godless people will be judged and destroyed.[13]

Those faithful to God will be saved from this destruction, taken away from the earth before it is destroyed. They will be *delivered* ⬚ [14] (⬚). By whom? The oracle bone writing of the character ⬚ leaves no doubt that it is the *Lamb* ⬚ (⬚) who is the *deliverer* and will *hide* ⬚ His people in that day. It will happen like this:

> The Lord Himself will come down from heaven. Those who have died believing in Christ [Jesus] will rise to life first; then we who are living at that time will be gathered up along with them in the clouds to meet the Lord in the air. And so we will always be with the Lord.[15]

deliver

Here is the answer to the question posed concerning death. There is a promised resurrection of all the faithful dead of all ages. Righteous people will live again (pp. 70,71)! We can know that God, the wise judge, will deal justly.

Some will be fortunate in not having to taste death at all— "we who are living at that time." These faithful ones will be taken directly to heaven on that day when Jesus returns. And what of the earth?

> But the Day of the Lord will come like a thief. On that Day the heavens will disappear with a shrill noise, the heavenly bodies will burn up and be destroyed, and the earth with everything in it will vanish.[16]

But ShangDi has promised a new earth after the destruction of the present one, with the eradication of sin and sinners. Jesus' disciple John, when an old man, related what he saw in a heavenly vision:

> Then I saw a *new heaven and a new earth*. The
> first heaven and the first earth disappeared, and the
> sea vanished. And I saw the Holy City, the new
> Jerusalem, coming down out of heaven from God,
> prepared and ready, like a bride dressed to meet
> her husband. I heard a loud voice speaking from
> the throne: "Now God's home is with mankind! He
> will live with them, and they shall be His people.
> God Himself will be with them, and He will be their
> God. He will wipe away all tears from their eyes.
> There will be no more death, no more grief or
> crying or pain. The old things have disappeared."[17]

God will make His dwelling place with people on the "new earth" which will then become the capital of the entire universe. His throne, will be in their midst. Rising above all in this beautiful celestial garden in the new Jerusalem is God's lofty throne on Mount Zion. The disciple John related more of his vision:

> The angel also showed me the river of the water of
> life, sparkling like crystal, and coming from the
> throne of God and of the Lamb and flowing down
> the middle of the city's street. On each side of the
> river is the tree of life, which bears fruit twelve
> times a year, once each month....

> The throne of God and of the Lamb will be in the
> city, and His servants will worship Him. They will
> see his face.... There shall be no more night ...
> because the Lord God will be their light, and they
> will rule as kings forever and ever.[18]

This earth and its human inhabitants have, since creation, been the object of ShangDi's greatest love and concern. Very soon, the lengthy controversy between ShangDi and the devil will be over. The war has already been decided. We must be on the right side—the winning side! God gives the invitation to all:

> Come, whoever is thirsty; accept the water of life as a gift, whoever wants it.[19]

There will be no more barrier at the garden *gate* 門 . All who have the Lamb's gift of *righteousness* 義 (義) may freely come and go into the new Garden of Eden. No one will be excluded from the *tree* 木 of life. Everyone may eat the fruit that gives everlasting life. Best of all, we can all *meet* 見 (見 , p. 39) face-to-face with ShangDi, as did Adam and Eve in the beginning.

> Blessed are those who do His commandments, that they may have the right to the tree of life, and may enter through the gates into the city.[20]

Furthermore, God promises,

> "To those who win the victory I will give the right to eat the fruit of the tree of life that grows in the Garden of God."[21]

Let the ancient Chinese characters speak truth to you. These must have been preserved in the earth for more than 4,000 years, until our very day, to convince us that ShangDi still lives. The great Sovereign of heaven, Creator of the earth, loves and has a vital interest in each individual.

> For I am certain that nothing can separate us from His love: neither death nor life, neither angels nor

other heavenly rulers or powers, neither the present nor the future, neither the world above nor the world below—there is nothing in all creation that will ever be able to separate us from the love of God which is ours through Christ Jesus our Lord.[22]

ShangDi

At last we can fully appreciate the oracle bone renderings of Di (ShangDi) 釆 [23] (帝). An amazing prophetic revelation is contained within the ancient script of His name.

But first we must re-examine 𠂇 (方 , p. 34), meaning *central focus, morally upright, pattern*. This character especially characterizes Jesus, the Son, in its definitions.

morally upright, central focus, pattern

Compare 𠂇 with 𢓥 (巫 , p. 26). Recall that we interpreted 𢓥 to indicate the three "God-Workers" of the Trinity as 𠂇𠂆 . In 𠂇 , we find the Trinity 𠂇𠂆 as three *Person(s)* 亻(人).

"God from above"

Consider again the graph 丅 (示 , p. 17) which also represents Jesus who came down from heaven. Now superimpose both 丅 and 𠂇 on the *tree* 木 , even as Jesus was nailed to the tree, the cross, He was the *central focus* and completed God's rescue plan for humanity. The cross became the tree of life for each of us: "[Christ] who Himself bore our sins in His own body on the tree."[24]

Lamb

And this is not all! We find other attributes of Christ in 釆 . Because of Jesus' love for us, He became the *fuel used in sacrifices* 尞 [25](尞). He was expended for us.

$$𠂇𠂆 \ + \ 亻 \ = \ 𠂇 \ + \ 木 \ + \ 尞 \ = \ 釆$$

Trinity   Person   Morally upright   tree fuel ShangDi

fuel used in sacrifices

The fact that He was expended for us becomes quite clear in the graph *Lamb* 羔 [26] (羔) where the *Lamb* 羊 (羊) of God, Jesus, is found as fuel in the *fire* 火 (火), or as the Sacrifice on the *mountain* 山 (山) of Calvary.

That Sacrifice, of course, was the *Person* 人 (人) from *above* 上 (上) who created our earth and mankind in the *beginning* 兀 (兀 , p. 17); the *perfect* | Person , the representative God 示 (示 , p. 17, 18) from *above* 上 ; that *noble* 大 (大) Man from heaven *above* 上 , the *God* 天 (天 , p. 16) who walked among men. **ShangDi is Jesus Christ!**

And so the true and original meaning of the Border Sacrifice to Heaven and identity of ShangDi are now fully revealed to us. **ShangDi is none other than Jesus Christ, our God and promised Savior, and the Border Sacrifice pointed to the atoning death of Jesus on the cross for the sins of the world.**

His name, ShangDi 帝 , was recorded and known to the earliest people of China's civilization, more than 4000 years ago. This is God's promise to all His people:

> "In every place where I record My name I will come to you, and I will bless you."[27]

There is just one more fact. This great, loving ShangDi / Jesus is still searching, yearning, and pleading for lost people everywhere to return to Him:

"Turn to Me now and be saved,
   people all over the world!
I am the only God there is.
My promise is true,
   and it will not be changed.
I solemnly promise by all that I am."[28]

Epilog

Synchronizing Chinese and Biblical History

How did the ancient Chinese acquire the same historical facts regarding creation, the temptation and fall of the first human couple, and a similar sacrificial worship system as the Hebrew people? We know that the Chinese did have this information from our previous study of their pictographic characters. How could two geographically widely-separated ancient peoples have such extensive identical data?

To answer these questions, we need to compare Chinese legends and the earliest Chinese dynastic records with the earth chronology recorded in the Bible. Contained within the first eleven chapters of Genesis (the first book of the Bible) are possible answers to the enigma. We will find that the early Chinese were contemporaries and descendants of the biblical man named Noah. In Genesis chapter 5 are detailed genealogies of earth's first inhabitants from which accurate chronological data can be accrued:

This is the book of the genealogy of Adam. In the
day that God created man, He made him in the
likeness of God. He created them male and female,
and blessed them and called them Mankind in the
day they were created. And Adam lived one hundred
and thirty years, and begot a son in his own likeness, after his image, and named him Seth. After he
begot Seth, the days of Adam were eight hundred
years; and he begot sons and daughters. So all the
days that Adam lived were nine hundred and thirty
years; and he died.

Seth lived one hundred and five years, and begot
Enosh. After he begot Enosh, Seth lived eight
hundred and seven years, and begot sons and
daughters. So all the days of Seth were nine hundred and twelve years; and he died.

Enosh lived ninety years, and begot Cainan. After he
begot Cainan, Enosh lived eight hundred and
fifteen years, and begot sons and daughters. So all
the days of Enosh were nine hundred and five years;
and he died. . . .[1]

For us, living on the verge of the 21st century A.D., the above
reads like a fairy tale. It would seem highly improbable that
Adam lived 930 years, Seth 912 years, and Enosh 905 years.
This certainly doesn't sound like today's life expectancy—and
it isn't. Evidently, their beautiful earth was completely free of
any life-shortening contamination and they themselves had
perfect bodies. Why should not early humans have lived nearly
1,000 years? In fact, according to Genesis, the life spans of the
first 10 generations of men averaged 912 years. But something
happened during the 10th generation.

> Then the Lord saw that the wickedness of man was great in the earth, and that every intent of the thoughts of his heart was only evil continually. And the Lord was sorry that He had made man on the earth, and He was grieved in His heart. So the Lord said, "I will destroy man whom I have created from the face of the earth, both man and beast, creeping thing and birds of the air, for I am sorry that I have made them." But Noah found grace in the eyes of the Lord.... Noah was a just man, perfect in his generations. Noah walked with God.[2]

Yet God waited another 120 years after making His drastic decision, while Noah and his three sons built a great ship, under divine direction, and preached righteousness to earth's evil inhabitants. However, these godly men met only derision from the world's wicked inhabitants. Finally, God sent a mighty worldwide flood to destroy all of earth's peoples, except for this man's family of eight persons (Noah, his wife, their sons, and their wives). Pairs of all kinds of animals also entered the ark prior to the flood and were likewise borne to safety through the deluge. From the accurate genealogical chronology of Adam's descendants recorded in the Bible, we know that the great flood took place 1656 years after creation.

Then, it was only 101 years after the flood (calculated from the genealogical data of Genesis, chapter 11) when another event of great importance took place. In the fifth generation after Noah, we read of this incident:

> To Eber [son of Salah, son of Arphaxad, son of Shem, son of Noah] were born two sons: the name of one was Peleg, for in his days the earth was divided.[3]

At the birth of this child, just 101 years after the flood, evil again abounded, so the Bible tells us "the earth was divided." If we read on, we learn what happened:

> Now the whole earth had one language and one speech. ... And they [men on the plain of Shinar in Mesopotamia] said, "Come, let us build ourselves a city, and a tower whose top is in the heavens; let us make a name for ourselves, lest we be scattered abroad over the face of the whole earth."

> But the Lord came down to see the city and the tower which the sons of men had built. And the Lord said, "Indeed the people are one and they all have one language, and this is what they begin to do; now nothing that they propose to do will be withheld from them. Come, let Us go down and there confuse their language, that they may not understand one another's speech." So the Lord scattered them abroad from there over the face of all the earth, and they ceased building the city. Therefore its name is called Babel, because there the Lord confused the language of all the earth; and from there the Lord scattered them abroad over the face of all the earth.[4]

At this very time, the varied languages of earth originated, including the Chinese language. In what year did this event take place? Our calendar reckonings used today are based upon the year of Christ Jesus' birth. The years before His birth are called "B.C." (before Christ), and the years after His birth, "A.D." (Latin, *anno Domini*, meaning "in the year of the Lord"). We have already stated that the flood took place 1656 years after creation. But how many years B.C. was this?

James Ussher (1581-1656), an Irish archbishop of Armagh, did a monumental study, gathering time-related biblical information and correlating this with known historically dated records. He concluded that the flood took place about 2348 B.C,[5] which would place the Tower of Babel incident, with the scattering of peoples over the earth, at about 2247 B.C.

We have examined Hebrew history as written in the Bible, so now let us look at the Chinese records. The establishment of China's first dynasty, the Xia dynasty in 2205 B.C., marks the historical beginning of China's 4,000 years of unbroken dynastic culture and civilization.

From the Shang dynasty (1766-1123 B.C.) to the Ch'ing dynasty (1644-1911 A.D.), the Chinese have traditionally regarded their own history and writing with reverence, believing that these relayed ancestral truths coming from divine or semi-divine origins. The connection between the written word and divine truth is revealed from the pictographic creation of the graph *to record, tell* written in two variant ways: [6] (曽). The first graph 曽 depicts a bound text of bamboo sticks ⊞⊞ , and a *mouth* ⊔ (口). The second graph shows the text ⊞⊞ and the "God Radical" 丅 (示). This certainly suggests that the source of the ancient *records* was inspired by God.

to record, tell

text

$$⊔ \quad + \quad ⊞⊞ \quad + \quad 丅 \quad = \quad 曽 , 丅⊞⊞$$

mouth (oral)	*text*	*God*		*to record*

Another oracle bone graph *law, statute* [7] (典)

law, statute

109

depicts revering hands 𝌆 lifting up the ancient texts 卌
(冊). This portrays the sacredness which early men had for
their written history. The first century *Shuo Wen* defines "tien"
(典) as "the Book of the Five Emperors," belonging to a
legendary period of prehistorical times.

The earliest surviving texts describing this ancient "Legendary Period" were written in the Zhou dynasty (1122-
255 B.C.), nearly 2,000 years *after* the events described. The
Zhou references relate in bits and pieces the myths and legends known at that time from even earlier texts and oral history. Of course there were inevitable distortion of facts by the
Zhou authors due to this 2,000 year lapse of time. But the
marvel of mythology is that its core of truth does indeed per-
petuate nonetheless. The traditional date (ca. 2800 B.C.) assigned to this legendary era stands on shakey ground if only
for the inconsistencies in various accounts.

Regardless, these historical legends provide valuable de-
scriptions of China's ancestral origins in terms of principal
sage heroes and their specific divine achievements. These ancient ancestors personified a wellspring of virtue, truth, laws
and inventions. The legendary period, in effect, was the foundation that birthed the Chinese civilization in 2205 B.C.

Therefore, the legends recorded in these Zhou texts are a
legitimate source for historical truth. Not surprisingly, they are
more reliable than the later Han dynasty texts which were often cluttered with imaginative detail and spinoffs influenced by
the later introduction of Taoist and Buddhist beliefs. The earli-

est mythologies appear in the Zhou texts, such as Nu-wa and the flood. They also describe the accomplishments of the ancient sage rulers—HuangDi, Yao, Shun, and Yu.[8] The popular creation story of Pan Gu appears later in a third century A.D. Han dynasty text (*Record of Cycles in Threes and Fives*), [　三五歷紀　].[9] The beginning of the Pan Gu narrative reveals a similar order of the Creation, as recorded in the Biblical Genesis:

- PAN GU: Heaven and earth were once inextricably commingled as a formless mass, from which Pan Gu originated.

  GENESIS 1: 2:   "The earth was without form and void;"

- PAN GU: After 18,000 years this formless mass split apart into bright and light, . . .dark and heavy.

  GENESIS 1: 4:   On the first day, God created light: "and God divided the light from the darkness."

- PAN GU: After another 18,000 years, heaven daily increased 10 feet in height, thus creating the space between the waters of the earth and the clouds.

  GENESIS 1: 7-8:   On the second day, God created heaven: "Thus God made the firmament, and divided the waters which were under the firmament from the waters which were above the firmament. . . .And God called the firmament heaven."

- PAN GU: The earth daily increased 10 feet in thickness

    GENESIS 1:9,10: On the third day, God created the dry land: "Then God said, 'Let the waters under the heaven be gathered together into one place, and let the dry land appear. . . .' And God called the dry land earth."

* PAN GU; Pan Gu, between the heaven and the earth daily increased ten feet in size.

    (Later texts add that after Pan Gu died, his breath became the wind and clouds, his voice the thunder, his left and right eyes the sun and moon, and from the remainder of this body came the mountains, rivers, plants and trees, etc., and finally man).

    GENESIS 1:11-27: On the fourth day, God created the lights in the heavens, and on the fifth day, birds of the air, and on the sixth day, He created the creatures of the land, and finally He created man.

While the Pan Gu creation story was written in the 3rd century A.D., the story of the Flood appeared as early as 1000 B.C. in the *Book of Odes (Shih Ching)*[10] [詩經] and the *Book of Documents (Shu Ching)*[11] [書經]. This latter contains the earliest writings in China, predating the oracle bone inscriptions. The Flood story was also the most pervasive of all other legends in ancient China. The *Shu Ching* records:

> The flood waters were everywhere, destroying everything as they rose above the hills and swelled up to Heaven.[11]

in the beginning

Perhaps the most striking testimony that the Chinese perceived their ancient origins as a people following this worldwide flood, is the graph [12] (昔) which means *in the beginning*. The graph shows the "flood waters" [13] (卌), meaning *disaster,* that, according to the Flood myth, "swelled up to Heaven," and here rises up to the *sun* (日). This obviously was no ordinary flood, but the unstoppable Flood which they believed occurred "at the beginning" of their history.

disaster (rising water)

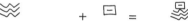

disaster (rising water)	+	sun	=	in the beginning

sun

Next, let us look at the story of Nu-wa (also written Nu-kua) and the flood. Nu-wa was a "divine" hero assigned traditionally to the Three sovereigns period at the beginning of the legendary era. The name "nu" (女) does not necessarily indicate a woman, but could have been his clan name since many of these were based on the feminine element. Nu-kua is mentioned in two Zhou dynasty texts, but the *Huai-nan-tzu,*

2nd century B.C. record tells the full story:

> In very ancient times, the four pillars [at the compass points] were broken down, the nine provinces [of the habitable world] were split apart, Heaven did not wholly cover [earth] and Earth did not completely support [Heaven]. Fires flamed wihout being extinguished, waters inundated without being stopped, fierce beasts ate the people, and birds of prey seized the old and weak in their claws. Thereupon Nu-kua fused together stones of the five colors with which to patch together azure heaven, and cut off the feet of a turtle to re-set the four pillars.[14]

A later source, the *Feng-su T'ung-yi ("Comprehensive Meaning of Customs")*,[15] tells us that Nu-kua was the creator of mankind and the one who instituted marriage: "Nu-kua created men by patting yellow earth together." This may have been a confused merging of the real creation of man from the earth, and the story of Noah (Nu-kua) as the progenitor of all mankind after the flood. While at first the above story seems to bear little resemblance to the Biblical flood narrative, let us look closely at the essentials of the story and compare.

NU-KUA OF CHINA	NOAH OF GENESIS
1. Similar pronunciation:	
"Nu-wa, Nu-kua" =	Noah
2. The four pillars [covenant] = on earth upholding heaven were broken down.	Genesis 6: 11 "The earth was corrupt before God."

3. The whole habitable world = Genesis 7:23"So He
   was destroyed by fires and destroyed all living
   an unstoppable flood. things which were on
   the face of the ground;
   ...and birds of the
   air."

4. The nine provinces [the = Genesis 8:2 "The foun-
   whole land] were split tains of the deep" rent
   apart [literally]. upheaval in the earth.

5. Nu-kua alone saved the = Genesis 6:8 "But Noah
   world when he patched found grace in the eyes
   the heavens. of the Lord."

6. Nu-kua restored the pillars = Genesis 9:9 God said,
   between heaven and earth. And as for Me, "be-
   hold, I establish My
   covenant between Me
   and with your seed..."

7. Stones of Five Colors = Genesis 9:13 "I set My
   patched the azure heaven. rainbow in the cloud,
   and it shall be for the
   sign of the covenant
   between me and the
   earth."

8. Nu-Kua "fashioned" = We are all ultimately
   mankind. descendants of Noah.

115

9. Nu-kua instituted marriage = Genesis 9:1 "So God
for men to propagate. blessed Noah and his
sons, and said to them,
'Be fruitful and multi-
ply, and fill the earth.'"

Then we come to HuangDi. To most Chinese minds, Emperor HuangDi represents the beginning of Chinese culture.
The event in China's history that turned it from a primitive to a
civilized society was HuangDi's defeat of two other powerful
figures in the first great battle in China's legendary history.
HuangDi is also credited with inventing the key hallmarks of
Chinese culture, such as bronze making, writing, the cross-
bow, rites, music and medical texts.[16] He is placed in the Period of the Five Emperors, a legendary period most historians
either discount or simply quote the "traditional" date of ca.
2800 B.C.

yellow

Huang Di is an important figure in China's origins, because
each of the founders of China's first three dynasties, the Xia,
the Shang, and the Zhou, all had claimed descendancy from
HuangDi. All three founders shared a beginning in this one
noble ancestor. Our earliest and most direct evidence of
HuangDi comes from the oracle bone graph representing his
name, *Huang, Yellow* 奥 [17](黃). The graph depicts a
great, noble 大 (大) man of the *garden* 田 (田). He is
a great man whose ancestral lineage is graphically linked to

God's creation of the *noble* 𠆢 man of the *garden* 田 ,
Adam. It becomes apparent from this graph 黃 that HuangDi,
the earliest known imperial ancestor, was identified as a lineal
descendant of Adam whom God created in the Garden.

𠆢   +   田   =   黃

noble (man)   *garden*   *Huang (Di)*

The founder of the Xia, Ruler Yu, with his predecessors Yao
and Shun of the "Five Emperor" legendary period, were historically revered as exemplars of moral uprightness. Shun, we
know, sacrificed to ShangDi (see p. 2) and Yu is the hero in
the Flood story as recorded in China. It describes how after
the Flood, Heaven sent the divine Kun to take care of the flood
waters, but it was not until Kun's son, Yu, devised a new tech-
nique to channel the waters out to sea, that the land was eventually made habitable.

If we are to believe this, and there is good reason to, then
up until 2205 B.C., this portion of the land in China was not
yet habitable. The supernatural ability of Yu, to make the land
habitable, caused Shun to turn over the rulership to Yu, thus
beginning China's first Xia dynasty. But what of the legendary
period before the Xia?

Archaeologists have long sought, but not yet found evidence
for the "Legendary Period." Neolithic villages lie just below
the level of the Shang dynasty. Some historians interpret this to
mean that the legendary period was in reality the Neolithic
period. But these excavated Neolithic cultures do not reveal

the writing, the bronzes, the chariots, etc, attributed to HuangDi.

The Bible tells us that there was a critical point in time, after the great flood, and after the re-population by Noah's descendants, when God cause a mighty dispersion of peoples and confusion of languages throughout the world. This was not simply a natural migration of peoples, but the supernatural power of God that brought to the whole world new languages, new peoples, new nations. Is it a coincidence that Bishop Ussher's date of this Tower of Babel dispersion, 2247 B.C., is so close to the traditional date, 2205 B.C., of China's first Xia dynasty?

Could it be that the Legendary Period recalls a time when the ancestors of China's first dynasties were indeed kin to Noah's descendants before the great dispersion of mankind over the earth?

Since all peoples of earth are descended from Noah or his sons, the early Chinese ancestors were likely contemporaries of Noah, who lived 350 years after the flood (Genesis 9: 28). Therefore, information could have been passed to them by word-of -mouth, even by Noah himself. He, in turn, obtained historical data from his father Lamech, who was 56 years old when Adam died.

Thus, all the details of creation and life before the flood could have been passed to the Chinese from Adam with only two intermediaries, Lamech and Noah. No wonder the Chinese ideographic characters, in which these historical narratives are stored, agree completely with the stories later recorded in

Genesis by Moses (a descendant of Eber, father of Peleg and patriarch of the Hebrews). The source of historical authenticity was the same for both the ancient Chinese and Moses.

References

1: Confucius Revealed the Clue, pp. 1-6

1. James Legge, *The Doctrine of the Mean,* XIX, 6., *The Chinese Classics,* Vol. I, p. 404. (Oxford: Clarendon Press, 1893). [Reprint: Taipei, SMC Publ. Inc., 1994].
2. James Legge, *The Shu Jing (Book of Historical Documents): The Books of Yu, 1,6, The Chinese Classics,* Vol. III, p. 33-34. (Oxford: Clarendon Press, 1893). [Reprint: Taipei, SMC Publ. Inc., 1994, 1991].
3. James Legge, *The Notions of the Chinese Concerning God and Spirits* (Hong Kong: Hong Kong Register Office, 1852), p 52.
4. *Ibid.,* pp. 24, 25.
5. *Ibid.,* p. 30.
6. *Ibid.,* p. 31.
7. *Ibid.,* pp.24, 25.

2: Who Is ShangTi?, pp.7-14

1. James Legge, *The Notions of the Chinese Concerning God and Spirits* (Hong Kong: Hong Kong Register Office, 1852), p. 28.
2. *Ibid.,* p. 29.
3. *Ibid.,* p. 29.
4. *Ibid.,* p. 30.
5. James Legge, *The Doctrine of the Mean,* XIX, 6, *The*

Chinese Classics, Vol. 1, p. 404. (Oxford: Clarendon Press, 1893). [Reprint: Taipei, SMC Publ. Inc., 1994, 1991].

6. *Ibid.,* p. 51.

7. Hsin Cheng Yu, *Ancient Chinese History* (Taipei: Taiwan Commercial Press, 1963), p. 6.

8. G. D. Wilder and J. H. Ingram, *Analysis of Chinese Characters* (Taipei: Chin Wen Publ. Co., 1964), pp. iv-vi.

9. Cheng Te-K'un, *Archaeology in China* (Cambridge, England: W. Heffer & Sons Ltd., 1960) Vol. 2, Shang China, p. 1.

10. Genesis 1:1-2, 9-10, 16, 27-28 NKJV.

11. Schuessler, Axel, *A Dictionary of Early Zhou Chinese* (Honolulu: University of Hawaii Press, 1987), p. 123, 528.

3: In the Beginning—God, pp. 15-22

1. James Legge, *The Notions of the Chinese Concerning God and Spirits* (Hong Kong: 1852), p. 28. [Reprint: Taipei, 1971]. [Hereafter abbreviated *Notions*]

2. Genesis 1:1 NKJV.

3. Lung Ch'uan Kuei T'ai Lang, *Shih Chi Hui Chu K'ao Cheng (Taipei: Han Ching Wen Hua Enterprise Co., Ltd., 1983), p. 497.*

4. Shih Chao, edit., *The Works of Motze* (Taipei: Wen Chih Publishing, 1976), p. 291.

5. Chung-kuo k'e-hsueh-yuan k'ao-ku yen-chiu-so, *Chia-Ku Wen-Pien* (Peking: K'ao-ku-hsueh chuan-k'an yi-chung ti-shih-ssu hao, 1965), no. 1.1. [Hereafter abbreviated CKWP]; Also, Chin Hsiang-heng, *Hsu Chia-Ku Wen Pien.* (Taipei: I wen yin shu kuan, 1959), no. 1.1 [Hereafter abbreviated HCKWP].

6. *CKWP,* no. 10.11; *HCKWP,* no. 10.16.

7. *CKWP,* no. 1.2; *HCKWP,* no. 1.1

8. *CKWP,* no. 1.2; *HCKWP,* no. 1.2.

9. *CKWP* , no. 1.3; *HCKWP,* no. 1.3.

10. *CKWP,* no. 3.2; *HCKWP,* no. 3.3.

11. *CKWP*, no. 1.1; *HCKWP*, no. 1.1.
12. *CKWP*, no. 8.1; *HCKWP*, no. 8.1.
13. John 1:1-3, 14 NKJV.
14. Revelation 1:8 NKJV.
15. *CKWP*, no. 11.11; *HCKWP*, no. 11.11.
16. *HCKWP*, no. 11.1.
17. Joel 2:23, 29 NKJV.
18. *HCKWP*, no. 11.14.
19. Acts 2:1-4 NKJV.
20. *Notions,* p. 29.
21. Psalm 33:6,9 TEV.
22. Genesis 1:24 NKJV.
23. *CKWP*, no. 6.8; *HCKWP*, no. 6.13.
24. *CKWP*, no. 2.6; *HCKWP*, no. 2.6.
25. *CKWP*, no. 2.7; *HCKWP*, no. 2.7.

4: Chinese Concepts of Mankind's Creation, pp. 23-30

1. Li Hsiao-ting, *Chia-Ku Wen-Tzu Chi Shih,* 8 vol. x (Nonkang: Chung-yang yen-chiu-yuan li-shih yu-yen yen-chiu-so, 1965), no. 3736. [Hereafter abbreviated *CKWT]*
2. *CKWP*, no. 10.7; *HCKWP*.no. 10.10.
3. Genesis 2:7.
4. *CKWP*, no. 13.7; *HCKWP*, no. 13.8.
5. *CKWT*, no. 159.
6. *HCKWP*, no. 13.8; *CKWP*, no. 4001.
7. Isaiah 64:8 NIV
8. *CKWP*, no. 10.16; *HCKWP*, no.10.23.
9. *CKWP*, no. 8.8; *HCKWP*, no. 8.11.
10. Genesis 1:31.
11. *CKWP*, no. 5.2; *HCKWP*, no. 5.3.
12. Ma Wei Ching, *Wei Ching Chia Ku Wen Yuan* (Yunlin: Ma Fu Distributor, 1971), p. 1297.
13. Psalm 104: 1-2 NKJV.
14. *CKWP*, no. 10.11; *HCKWP*, no. 10.15.
15. *CKWP*, no. 10.7; *HCKWP*, no. 10.10.
16. Psalm 8:5 NRSV.

17. *CKWP,* no. 9.2; *HCKWP,* no. 9.2.
18. *CKWP,* no. 9.4; *HCKWP,* no. 9.4.
19. *CKWP,* no. 3.10.
20. *HCKWP,* no. 3.36.
21. Genesis 2:10 NKJV..
22. *HCKWP,* no. 13.11.
23. Genesis 2:19-20 TEV.
24. Genesis 2:18 TEV.
25. Genesis 2:21-22 TEV.
26. *CKWP,* no 12.10; *HCKWP,* no. 12.12.
27. *CKWP.* 12.4; *HCKWP,* no. 12.12.
28. Genesis 2:24 NIV.
29. *CKWP,* no. 10.17; *HCKWP,* no. 10.23.
30. Genesis 1:28 RSV.
31. Genesis 2:25.
32. *CKWP,* no. 10.9; *HCKWP,* no. 10.12.
33. *CKWP,* no. 10.7; *HCKWP,* no. 10.10.
34. *CKWP,* no. 7.23; *HCKWP,* no. 7.25.
35. *CKWP,* no. 7.23; *HCKWP,* no. 7.24.
36. *HCKWP,* no. 14.13.
37. *CKWP,* no. 7.16; *HCKWP,* no. 7.17.
38. *CKWP,* no. 7.19; *HCKWP,* no. 7.21.
39. *CKWP,* no. 14.7; *HCKWP,* no. 14.10.
40. Genesis 2:1-3 NIV.
41. *CKWP,* no. 7.17; *HCKWP,* no. 7.18.
42. *CKWP,* no. 14.8; *HCKWP,* no. 14.10.

5: Secrets of a Lost Garden, pp. 31-40

1. Genesis 2:8-10 RSV.
2. *CKWP,* no. 13.9; *HCKWP,* no. 13.11.
3. Schuessler, Axel, *A Dictionary of Early Zhou Chinese* (Honolulu: University of Hawaii Press, 1987), p. 126.
4. James Strong, *The New Strong's Exhaustive Concordance of the Bible* (Nashville: Thomas Nelson Publ. , 1990) "Hebrew and Chaldee Dictionary," # 5731, p. 85.

5. *CKWP.* no. 2.28; *HCKWP,* no. 2.31.
6. *HCKWP,* no. 9.6.
7. *Ibid,* no. 11.3
8. *CKWP,* no. 11.9; *HCKWP,* no. 11.10.
9. *CKWP,* no. 11.10; *HCLWP,* no. 11.10.
10. *Ibid.*
11. *HCKWP,* no. 11.1.
12. Genesis 2:9.
13. *CKWP,* no. 6.5; *HCKWP,* no. 6.6.
14. *HCKWP,* no. 9.6.
15. *CKWP,* no. 10.8; *HCKWP,* 10.12.
16. *CKWP,* no. 8.11; *HCKWP,* no. 8.17.
17. *HCKWP,* no. 2.26.
18. Psalm 36:6-9 RSV
19. Genesis 2:16-17.
20. *CKWP,* no. 7.10; *HCKWP,* no. 7.10.
21. Hebrews 12:29.
22. *CKWP,* no. 6.3; *HCKWP,* no. 6.3.
23. *CKWP,* no. 6.6; *HCKWP,* no. 6.8.
24. *CKWP,* no. 2.14; *HCKWP,* no. 2.15.
25. *CKWP,* no. 13.10; *HCKWP,* no. 13.13.
26. *CKWP,* no. 13.10.
27. Jeremiah 27:5 NIV.
28. *CKWP,* no. 13.11; *HCKWP,* no. 13.13.
29. *CKWP,* no. 13.11; *HCKWP,* no. 13.13.
30. Psalm 33:9.
31. *CKWP,* no. 13.10; *HCKWP,* no. 13.12.
32. Genesis 2:15 NKJV.
33. *CKWP,* no. 2.15; *HCKWP,* no. 2.15.
34. *CKWP,* no. 14.5; *HCKWP,* no. 14.7.
35. *CKWP,* no. 14.4; *HCKWP,* no. 14.6.
36. *CKWP,* no. 9.6; *HCKWP,* no. 9.6
37. *CKWP,* no. 4131.

38. Psalm 24:3-5 RSV..
39. *CKWP,* no. 12.3.
40. *CKWP.* no. 12.3; *HCKWP,* no.12.4.
41. *CKWP,* no. 8.15; *HCKWP,* 8.23.
42. *CKWP,* no.4.1; *HCKWP,* no. 4.1.
43. *CKWP,* no. 4.3; *HCKWP,* no. 4.2

6: Invader in the Garden, pp. 41-46

1. *HCKWP,* no. 10.9.
2. Ezekiel 28: 12-13, 15-17 NIV.
3. Isaiah 14:12-14 NIV.
4. Revelation 12:7-9 RSV.
5. Genesis 2:16-17.
6. *CKWP,* no. 6.9; *HCKWP,* no. 6.13.
7. *CKWP,* no. 5.7; *HCKWP,* no. 5.10.
8. *CKWP,* no. 2.7; *HCKWP,* no. 2.7
9. *CKWT* no. 3207.
10. *CKWP,* no. 8.10; *HCKWP,* no. 8.14.
11. Genesis 3:1 TEV.
12. Genesis 3:2-3 TEV.
13. Genesis 3:4 NIV.
14. *HCKWP,* no. 12.17.
15. Genesis 3:5 NIV.

7: The Fatal Bite, pp. 47-54

1. Genesis 3:6 NKJV.
2. *CKWP,* no. 12.10; *HCKWP,* no. 12.12.
3. Genesis 3:6.
4. *CKWP,* no. 12.21; *HCKWP,* no. 12.28.
5. Genesis 3:6 RSV.
6. *CKWP,* no. 3.1; *HCKWP,* no. 3.1.
7. *CKWP,* no. 2.19; *HCKWP,* no. 2.22.
8. Genesis 3:7 RSV.
9. Genesis 3:7 RSV.

10. *CKWP,* no. 8.9; *HCKWP,* no. 8.12.
11. Genesis 3:8-9 TEV.
12. Genesis 3:11 TEV.
13. *CKWP,* no. 4.19; *HCKWP,* no. 4.23.
14. Genesis 3:12-13 TEV.
15. Genesis 3:15 NKJV.
16. *CKWP,* no. 13.14; *HCKWP,* no. 13.5.
17. *CKWP,* no. 12.7; *HCKWP,* no. 12.10.
18. *HCKWP,* no. 14.17.
19. *CKWP,* no. 4.21.
20. *CKWP,* no. 3.29; *HCKWP,* no. 3.32.
21. *CKWP,* no. 4.21; *HCKWP,* no. 4.26.
22. Genesis 3:16 NKJV.
23. *CKWP,* no. 6.9; *HCKWP,* no. 6.15.
24. Genesis 3:17, 19 NIV.
25. *CKWP,* no. 6.5; *HCKWP,* no. 6.6.
26. *HCKWP,* no. 14.13.
27. *CKWP,* no. 2.15.
28. *CKWP,* no. 2667.
29. *CKWP,* no. 6.9; *HCKWP,* no. 6.14.
30. Genesis 3:19 NIV.

8: A Costly Rescue Plan, pp. 55-62

1. Genesis 3:22-24 NIV.
2. Lung Kuang Lan, *P'ing An We P'u* (Taipei: *Decision Magazine,* Decemaber 1985), p. 15.
3. *CKWP,* no. 12.3; *HCKWP,* no. 12.4.
4. *CKWP,* no. 12.14; *HCKWP,* no. 12.15.
5. *CKWP,* no. 9.6; *HCKWP,* no. 9.6. For its ancient meaning "alien," see Shen Chien-shi, "An Essay on the Primitive Meaning of the Character *Kuei,*" translated by Ying Ch'ien-li, *Monumenta Serica* II, no. 1 (1936-37), pp. 1-20.
6. *HCKWP,* no. 3.10.
7. *CKWP,* no. 9.6; *HCKWP,* no. 9.6.
8. Genesis 3:21 NIV.

9. *CKWP*, no. 4.22; *HCKWP*, no. 4.27.
10. *Ibid.*
11. *CKWP*, no. 8.2; *HCKWP*, no. 8.4.
12. *HCKWP*, no. 8.13.
13. *CKWP*, no. 4.13; *HCKWP*, no. 4.12.
14. John 1:29 NKJV.
15. *CKWP*, no. 12.18; *HCKWP*, no. 12.23.
16. *CKWP*, no. 12.18; *HCKWP*, no. 12.22.
17. *CKWP*, no. 12.14; *HCKWP*, no. 12.18.
18. *CKWP*, no. 4.14; *HCKWP*, no. 4.14.
19. *CKWP*, no. 10.8; *HCKWP*, no. 10.11.
20. Genesis 3:24 NKJV.
21. Exodus 25:22 NKJV.
22. Psalm 80:1 NKJV.
23. *CKWP*, no. 2.8; *HCKWP*, no. 2.8.
24. *CKWP*, no. 12.3; *HCKWP*, no. 12.5.
25. *CKWP*, no. 1.4.
26. *CKWP*, no. 5.14; *HCKWP*, no. 5.17.
27. *CKWP*, no. 1735.
28. *CKWP*, no. 2.3; *HCKWP*, no. 2.3.
29. Leviticus 9:2 RSV.
30. Genesis 4:2-5 NIV.
31. *CKWP*, no. 2421.
32. *CKWP*, no. 8.13; *HCKWP*, no. 8.20.
33. Genesis 4:15 RSV.
34. Genesis 4:16 NIV.

9: Confucius Pointed the Way, pp. 63-72

1. Genesis 3:24 RSV.
2. *CKWP*, no. 10.15; *HCKWP*, no. 10.21.
3. 1 Corinthians 15:47.
4. *CKWP*, no. 10.14; *HCKWP*, no. 10.20.
5. *Ibid.*
6. *HCKWP*, no. 6.2.
7. *CKWP*, no. 7.1; *HCKWP*, no. 7.1.
8. Psalm 51:16-17 NIV.

9. James Legge, *The Chinese Classics*, Vol. I-V (Reprint, Taipei: SMC Publishing Inc., 1994), Vol. III: The Shoo King, [Chou Shu, 1.7], p. 286.
10. *Ibid.*, Vol. IV: The She King [Part IV, 4.2], p. 623.
11. *Ibid.*, Vol. IV: The She King [Part III, Book I, 7.7], p. 454.
12. *Ibid.*, Vol. I: Confucian Analects [XX.3], p. 354.
13. *Ibid.*, Vol. I: Confucian Analects [II.4], p. 146-7.
14. *Ibid.*, Vol. IV: The She King [Part III, Book III, 1.1], p. 505.
15. *Ibid.*, Vol. IV: The She King [Part II, Book V, 4.1] p. 340.
16. *Ibid.*, Vol. I: Confucian Analects [III.13], p. 159.
17. *Ibid.*, Vol. I: Confucian Analects [VII.33], p. 206.
18. *Ibid.*, Vol. I: Confucian Analects [VII.21], p. 202.
19. *Ibid.*, Vol. I: Confucian Analects [VII.22], p. 202.
20. *Ibid.*, Vol. I: The Doctrine of the Mean [XIX.6], p. 404.
21. Psalm 104:29-30 NIV.
22. Psalm 146:4 RSV.
23. Daniel 12:2-3 RSV.
24. Isaiah 53 TEV.

10: The Seed of the Woman, pp. 73-82

1. Luke 1:30-33 TEV.
2. Luke 1:34 TEV.
3. Luke 1:34-35 TEV.
4. Luke 1:38 TEV.
5. Matthew 1:20-21 TEV.
6. Luke 2:10-12 TEV.
7. Matthew 2:2 TEV.
8. Micah 5:2,4-5 TEV.
9. Matthew 2:8 TEV.
10. Luke 2:46-50 TEV.
11. Luke 2:40 TEV.
12. John 1:29 TEV.

13. 1 Corinthians 11:23-24 TEV.
14. Matthew 26:28 TEV.
15. *CKWP,* no. 5.11; *HCKWP,* no. 5.14.

11: Original Purpose of the Altar of Heaven, pp. 83-92

1. Matthew 26:61 TEV.
2. Matthew 26:63 TEV.
3. Luke 23:3-4 TEV.
4. Luke 23:14-16 TEV.
5. Matthew 27:24 TEV.
6. Hebrews 13:12 RSV.
7. Luke 23:34 TEV.
8. Matthew 1:23
9. Matthew 1:21 NKJV.
10. Mark 15:34 NIV.
11. 2 Corinthians 5:21 NKJV.
12. John 19:30 NIV.
13. Matthew 27:51-53 TEV.
14. R. H. Mathews, *Chinese-English Dictionary* (Cambridge, MA: Harvard University Press, thirteenth printing, 1975), p. 1167.
15. John 8:12 TEV.
16. John 1:9 NKJV.
17. 1 John 1:10, 11 NKJV.
18. *CKWP,* no. 2.5; *HCKWP,* no. 2.5.
19. Zechariah 13:1 NKJV.
20. *CKWP,* no. 11.10.
21. Revelation 22:17.
22. John 3:16 RSV.
23. Matthew 26:26, 28 TEV.
24. John 2:19 NIV.
25. 1 Corinthians 15:22 TEV.
26. Luke 24:50 NIV.
27. Acts 1:8 TEV.
28. Acts 1:11 TEV.

12: ShangDi's Last Promise

1. John 14:1-3, 6 TEV.
2. Revelation 21:10-19.
3. Revelation 22:1-2.
4. Revelation 14:1, 3 NKJV.
5. Psalm 99:1-2 NKJV.
6. John 1:1-4, 10-12, 14 TEV.
7. John 10:30 TEV.
8. John 14:8-10 NIV.
9. *HCKWP*, no. 12.25.
10. *CKWP*, no. 12.20; *HCKWP*, no. 12.25.
11. Matthew 24:3 NKJV.
12. Matthew 24 NKJV.
13. 2 Peter 3:3-4, 7 TEV.
14. Ma Wei Ching, *Wei Ching Chia Ku Wen Yuan*, (Yunlin: Ma Fu Distributor 1971), no 1283.
15. 1 Thessalonians 4:16-17 TEV.
16. 2 Peter 3:10 TEV.
17. Revelation 21:1-4 TEV.
18. Revelation 22:1-5 TEV.
19. Revelation 22:17 TEV.
20. Revelation 22:14 NKJV.
21. Revelation 2:7 TEV.
22. Romans 8:38-39 TEV.
23. *HCKWP*, no. 1.1.
24. 1 Peter 2:24 NKJV.
25. *CKWP*, no. 10.7; *HCKWP*, no. 10.10.
26. *CKWP*, no. 4.13; *HCKWP*, no. 4.13.
27. Exodus 20:24 NKJV.
28. Isaiah 45:22-23 TEV.

Epilog: Synchronizing Chinese and Biblical History

1. Genesis 5:1-11 NKJV.
2. Genesis 6:5-9 NKJV.

3. Genesis 10:25 NKJV.
4. Genesis 11:1, 4-9 NKJV.
5. F. C. Thomson, *A Complete System of Biblical Studies, The New Chain Reference Bible*, (Indianapolis: B. B. Kirkbride Bible Co., Inc., 1964), p. 186 (no. 4222b).
6. *CKWP*, no. 5.3; *HCKWP*, no. 5.6.
7. *HCKWP*, no. 2.34.
8. *HCKWP*, no. 5.2.
9. *Shih Ching and Shu Ching* (also called Shang Shu).
10. Wang Hsiao-lien, *Chung-Kuo Ti Shen Hua Shih-Chieh.* (Taipei: shih-pao wen-hua ch'u-pan ch'i-yeh you-hsien kung-ssu, 1987), p. 485.
11. James Legge, *The Chinese Classics*, Vol. III: Shoo King [T'ang shu, Yao-tien, Part I, Chapter 3.11], p. 24.
12. *CKWP*, no. 7.2; *HCKWP*, no. 7.3.
13. *HCKWP*, no. 11.10.
14. LiuWen-tien, *Huai Nan Hung Lieh chi Chieh.* (Shanghai: Shang wu, 1923; Taipei repreint, 1968), Chapter VI, 10a.11.
15. Wu Shu-ping, *Feng Su Tung I Chiao Shih.* (T'ien-chin shih: T'ien-chin jen min ch'u pan she, 1980), p. 449.
16.
17. *CKWP*, no. 13.10; *HCKWP*, no. 13.13.
18. James Legge, *The Chinese Classics*, Vol. III: Shoo King [Part II, 4.1], p. 76.

Bibliography

Bodde, Derk, "Myths of Ancient China," in *Mythologies of the Ancient World*, ed. Samuel N. Kramer. New York: Doubleday, 1961.

Chin Hsiang-hen, *Hsu Chia-Ku Wen Pien*. Taipei: 1959 (Reprint: I-wen Yin-shu-kuan ch'u-pan, 1993).

Ching, Julia, *Confucianism and Christianity*. Tokyo, New York and San Francisco: Kodansha International, 1977.

Legge, James, *The Chinese Classics*, Vol. I: *Confucian Analects* and *The Doctrine of the Mean*, Vol. III: *The Shoo King*, Vol. IV: *The She King*. Oxford: Clarendon Press, 1893. (Reprint, Taipei: SMC Publishing Inc., 1991, 1994).

Legge, James, *The Notions of the Chinese Concerning God and Spirits*. Hong Kong: Hong Kong Register Office, 1852.

Li Hsiao Ting, *Chia Ku Wen Tzu Chi Shih*. Thesis No. 50, Chung-yang yen-chiu-yuan li-shih yu-yen yen-chiu-suo, 1965).

Liu Wen-tien, *Huai Nan Hung Lieh Chi Chieh* Shanghai: Shang wu, 1923. (Reprint, Taipei, 1968).

Lung Ch'uan Kuei T'ai Lang, *Shih Chi Hui Chu K'ao Cheng*. (Taipei: Han ching wen-hua shih-yeh you-hsien kung-ssu ch'u pan, 1983).

Mathews, R. H., *Chinese-English Dictionary*. Cambridge, MA: Harvard University Press, thirteenth printing, 1975.

Ma Wei Ching, *Wei Ching Chia Ku Wen Yuan*. Yunlin: Ma fu Distributor, 1972.

Schuessler, Axel, *A Dictionary of Early Zhou Chinese.* Honolulu: University of Hawaii Press, 1987.

Sun Hai-po, ed., *Chia Ku Wen Pien* (Beijing: Chung-kuo
k'e-hsueh-yuan k'ao-ku yen-chiuo-so, 1965).

Thompson, Frank C., *A Complete System of Biblical Studies, The New Chain Reference Bible.* Indianapolis: B. B.
Kirkbride Bible Co., 1964.

Wang Hsiao-lien, *Chung-Kuo Ti Shen-Hua Shih-Chieh.
(Taipei: Shih-pao wen-hua ch'u-pan ch'i-yeh you-hsien
kung-ssu, 1987).*

Wilder, G. D., and Ingram, J. H., *Analysis of Chinese Characters.* Taipei: Chin Wen Publ. Co., 1964.

Wu Shu-p'ing, *Feng Su T'ung I chiao Shih* (Tianchin:
T'ianchin jen-min ch'u-pan she, 1980).

Character (Oracle Bone) Index

Pagination cited is for the first appearance of each character in the text. All characters follow dictionary (or most original, authentic) definitions except for an occasional definition, placed in quotes, assigned by the authors.

Character	Dictionary Equivalent	Page
夭 夭	Heaven, God, Tian	16
帝 帝	Di, (ShangDi), Supreme God	16. 102
丁 丁 示	to manifest, show, "God radical"	16, 33,102
二	above	16
丨	complete, perfect	17
勹 勹 勹	person	17, 56
元	first, head, beginning	17
雨	rain, "Holy Spirit"	18
雨	raindrops, "Holy Spirit"	19
◇	"holy"	19,24,32,81
屮	produce, bring forth, create	21
屮	"God"	21, 27, 39, 40
一	"ground, dust, earth"	21
口	mouth, person	21

	speak, tell	21
	great, noble, adult	23
	foundation	23
	fire	24, 29, 32
	"flame, holy"	24,36
	earth, clay, dust	24
	adult male person, scholar	24
	holy	25
	hand(s) ("God's)	25, 28,56
	create, found, start, to stand	25
	great, good	25
	work, artisan	26
	Worker of magic	26
	naked, red	26
	"kneeling man"	27,64
	imprint	27
	large, wide, garden, father	27
	field, garden	27,31
	woman	28
	suitable, to prepare	28
	to unite, join	29
	light, bare, naked	29
	palace	29
	roof	29
	adult person	29
	to follow, honor, religion	30
	six	30

㲃	to rest in	30
十	seven	30
⼻	to walk, travel, path	32
⼻	to overflow, spread out	32
川	river	32
山 火	mountain, fire	32
洲	region, island in a stream	32
泉	spring, source, fountain	33
木 林	tree, trees	33
焚	burning	33
中 中	center, place, morally upright	34,102
⼻	to walk with, near to, depend on	34
桼	rich, full, awe-inspiring	35,43
休	to rest, be happy	36
桑	mulberry tree	36
桼	to die, lose, ruin	36,48
男	male, feudal title	36
丿 乃	power, strength	36
劦 協	united in accord	37
畯	field supersivor	37
止	to stop, rest	38,48,50,53
降	to descend	38,49
厂 厂	cliff	38,39
阜	hill	39
阜 阝 阝	mount	38,39
聲	sound, voice	39
耳 耳	ear	39,60

have an audience with, meet	39
eye	39
watch over, observe	40
be near to, follow closely	41
restrain, bind	44
imperial decree	44
command, mandate	45
"mouth" (God's)	45
foreigner, kill, exterminate	45
representative of the dead	45
negative, no, not	46
desire, covet	48
strong, violent	48
disobedient	48
rebel, act contrary to	48
to walk	48
clothes, garment	49
to cover	49
stumble, fall	50
snake	51
seed, offspring, son	51
good	51
death	51
bad wicked	51
to foretell	51
distress, difficulty, trouble	52
enclosure	52

thorns	53
in due course, subsequent series	53
to mourn	53
because, reason, death	53
gate	56
alone	56
alien	56
strange, different	56
dread, fear	56
beginning	57
knife	57
depend, regard with favor	58
to die	58
hand (man's)	58
sheep	58
righteousness	58
lance, spear	58
me, I	58
beautiful	59
fiery, glorious	59
to ask, inquire	60
to sacrifice	60
blood	60
Lord, Master, God	60,81
bullock, ox	61,89
cruel, violent, fierce	61
elder brother	61

	"mark"	62
	boundary, border	64
	grasp, take hold of	64
	rejoice, give thanks to	64
	bright as the shining sun	65
	sun, light	65,113
	vessel	81
	sacrificial animals	89
	eternal	90
	place	97
	hide, conceal	97,99
	deliver	99
	fuel used in sacrifices	102
	lamb	103
	to record, tell	109
	text	109
	law, statute	109
	in the beginning	113
	disaster, "rising waters"	113
	yellow, Huang	116

If you enjoyed this book you will also want to obtain the following from your favorite bookseller:

Oracle Bones Speak is the bilingual version of *God's Promise to the Chinese:* English on the left side and Chinese on the right side of the spread. Beautifully illustrated!

The Beginning of Chinese Characters (Ethel R. Nelson, Richard Broadberry and Samuel Wang). A further careful analysis of Chinese radicals: oracle bone, bronzeware, traditional, and simplified, with definitions, analyses and comparisons with the Hebrew Scriptures. This book shows the over-whelming number of radicals which parallel the biblical Genesis.

God and the Ancient Chinese (Samuel Wang and Ethel R. Nelson). Not only Chinese characters parallel the ancient scriptures! In this book, Drs. Wang and Nelson study the ancient Chinese recitations and writings, comparing them to the Hebrew Scriptures.

Quest for the Holy Mountain (Ethel Nelson). Dr. Nelson's fascination with the "Holy Mountain" of Scripture as well as many of the world religions and in China render some fascinating results!

www.GenesisOfChineseCharacters.com